The Ultimate Prompt Book for Visual Artists

A reference book every artist needs

By Rosa Lozano

The Ultimate Prompt Book for Visual Artists Copyright © 2021 by Rosa Lozano. ALL RIGHTS RESERVED.

No part of this book may be reproduced or transmitted in any form by any means, electronic or mechanical, including photocopying and recording, or by any information storage and retrieval system, without the prior permission of the publisher. Commercial use of any/all of this book requires written permission and any licensing fees, if applicable, from the author, Rosa Lozano.
The information in this book is true and complete to the best of our knowledge. All recommendations are made without guarantee on the part of the author. The author disclaim any liability in connection with the use of this information.

All art, including front cover art and interior page illustrations are made by Rosa Lozano

ISBN: 9798596301625

TABLE OF CONTENTS

INTRODUCTION 4-5
CH. 1 Creativity Crash Course.. 6-10
CH. 2. Creative Techniques... 11-27
CH. 3 Lists of Projects... 28-31
CH. 4 Tools for visual artists... 32-34
CH. 5 People.. 35-49
CH. 6 Animals... 50-60
CH. 7 Nature... 61-76
CH. 8. Objects... 77-100
CH. 9 Places 101-106
CH. 10 Themes... 107-123
CH. 11 Color... 124-128
CH. 12 Stories... 129-139
BIBLIOGRAPHY 140-141

Introduction

Have you ever been staring at a blank page with a pencil ready to start but nothing comes out? I do. I think it's because I'm afraid I'm going to mess up the page with my drawings. That's a lot of time wasted and some of us don't have a lot of time. As artists, we need to develop our craft every single day in order to improve. But, in order to do that, we need a system.

This book is made of prompts and lists that were originally developed for my reference in my art projects. I compiled those lists in this book in order to help other artists. They save time and are great to keep creativity flowing. I kept the lists simple so that any artist can use them. They are divided in categories like people, nature, animals, objects and places.

This book is a place for reference, so whenever you are in need of an idea, open this book and you'll find one. Just flipping through this book could help you in generating ideas. Feel free to add items to the lists! The lists could be infinite.

I hope you will find something to create today. Never get stuck on what to draw again. Get ready to be inspired!

IDEAS TO USE THE PROMPT LISTS IN THIS BOOK

1. Every list is numbered so is easy to pick numbers to play around combining different elements.
2. Read the word and brainstorm what you know about the word. Brainstorm up to 20--50 items.
3. Research and explore the topic in question.
4. Keep adding to the list. This lists could be endless, this book it's just a starting point.
5. Some lists go up to 31 so you can do a monthly challenge where you have something to draw for the day.

Chapter 1
Creativity Crash Course

Welcome to Creativity class!

When I was in high school, I took a marketing class where the final project was coming up with an invention and selling it. Yes, an invention. They told us to come up with a brand-new, never seen before, unique creation. It was the final project. The class is famous and highly regarded in my hometown because some people have created exciting inventions, like a type of beer mix and a mixture of mayonnaise and mustard. Those inventions are still used here to this day! Naturally, I was excited to take the class; I have always loved to develop ideas and be creative since I was very young; around that time, I have just taken a course in comic books and character design, so I thought this was just right up in my alley.

To my surprise, the class didn't focus on the creative aspect of the invention or how to develop it; it was a more marketing-focused class. The whole experience was a disaster for me, at least. I was stuck and out of ideas because I didn't even know where to start. I couldn't come up with a single thought. How naive of me that I thought they were going to show us the process of how to come up with ideas. In the end, the help never came; it was a "swim or drown" kind of situation. I learned a lot about selling a product, but I didn't know how to be creative or develop my own and new ideas, which was the most crucial part.

What was my invention? Well, it was one of my teammates who came up with the product. She came up with a cotton pad with a sticky part for sanitizing public telephones by sticking it to the telephone handle. I mean, excellent, it got the job done; I learned that pressure is another way to develop ideas.

Ideas

For any creative endeavor, one needs to come up with new ideas all the time. It's hard, especially at the beginning, because no one teaches us how to do that. It's a personal discovery. But, there are techniques that you can start applying right now that could help you be more creative in an instant. You don't have to reinvent the wheel!

I have read so many books on creativity. I have collected notebooks and sketchbooks with notes and ideas on how to be creative. I've spent too many days searching for ways to achieve this, and what I have found is that anybody can be creative, and anybody can learn how to use these simple techniques. You don't need talent; you need action.

Learning from others

Ideas are very precious and finite; most artists will not tell you how they come up with ideas; they want to keep it a secret. And for a good reason! It takes time and effort. If we taught creativity in school as we teach math and science, we would live in a different world. Don't you think?

Beginner artists tend to think that the less they see other artists' artwork, the more they will have original ideas, which is crazy to me. One of my favorite pastimes is looking at sketchbooks from different artists on the internet. The simple act of scrolling and flipping through sketchbook artbooks one after the other makes me think about all the possibilities in my artwork. If someone else did it, probably you can too.

I don't believe that creativity is for the talented and the geniuses. Yes, some people are born naturally skilled in specific life areas, but they still have to put on some effort to make this a skill worthwhile.

My goal is to teach anyone how to be creative. If more people would take the time to learn it, think of all the inventions that we can come up with to make our lives easier. We would have many new designs each year in all aspects of our life; we wouldn't wait for someone else to make things up. Being creative shouldn't be just for the privileged and the naturally talented. It should be for everyone. Our brain is more powerful than we think it is.

I believe that every creative person has a system. Professional artists need to come up with stuff all the time. They know themselves well and therefore know where to get the inspiration. They go to places where they get inspired the most. Maybe they keep a favorite playlist on their phones. Or they try to do something different each day, and so on. Most importantly, they do the work and put the extra effort to keep their ideas flowing, so they know what to do when they want to be creative again.

Artists and scientists have a standard feature, they question everything and write everything down. One famous example would be Leonardo Da Vinci. We call him the Renaissance Man, meaning he did it all; he was a painter, inventor, and scientist. Lucky for us, he left his thoughts and drawings in sketchbooks. He questioned everything and kept a sketchbook where he recorded ideas and questions. Did he write because he was a genius? Did he was a genius because he wrote everything down?

Most artists know where to look to ignite their creativity. They take notes. Most of them have a routine that works for them. They know what to do to get them inspired.

Creativity is a skill that we need to develop, like riding a bike or learning how to cook. Most people do not think that they can be creative, so they tend to say things like, "I don't have ideas" or "I am not talented." Those statements are false. We all think ideas all of the time! When we put our minds to work, we can do a lot. I think we can all achieve a creative life if we make an effort. Anything good in life needs work.

My method

At first, coming up with ideas can be daunting. Once you get in the flow and know where to begin, you'll love it. You'llYou'll see there is a method for the madness: Lists!

I have collected numerous lists throughout my years of being an artist. Whenever I need a boost, I choose a prompt from one of my multiple lists. A prompt will usually make me draw even more and look for more ideas to draw. I pull around 30 to 40 pictures from each prompt (in post-its notes), and I keep those drawings in my monthly notebook. Every weekend I revise all the ideas I posted in my notebook and decide what I want to do with them. Maybe I'll make a digital illustration or an art journal page or a watercolor painting; who knows; the possibilities are endless!

Chapter 2
Creative Techniques

Techniques are guidelines to help us get to a specific goal. They are a set of instructions but, you can modify them as you wish and use them in other fields or other areas of interest. They make your work more original.

Everything has a technique, and the creative process is no exception. Artists have many innovative techniques at their disposal.

I've compiled several techniques for you to try on. The main focus is to get you out of your comfort zone and erase creative blocks. Artists use methods in creative settings like animation studios and visual development. But they also use it in different types of environments.

Keep these techniques close to you, try them, and modify them to your liking.

Look at the techniques in this book and make an effort to try them all. They are simple but probably will open your eyes to the endless ways you can achieve creativity.

Many books teach you different techniques, with step-by-step guides. Indeed, I use the methods I describe in the next pages. I use them regularly, and I am sure that they work.

I have collected them in this book, and I want to share the ones that have made me be a more original creator. Once you start looking for ideas, your brain will come up with more even while you sleep, so I advise you to read them all.

List of Creative Practical Techniques

- Keep an Idea Notebook
- Lists
- Combining Ideas
- Brainstorming
- Setting Limits
- Challenges
- Mind mapping
- Asking Questions
- Make intentional mistakes
- Metaphors
- Concepts
- Research a Random Topic
- Adding
- Subtracting
- Taking apart
- Pick something random and mix and match

Keeping a Notebook

Observe. Record. Research. Experiment. Please write it down. Anything goes in your notebook. There are no limits, even if it's something that doesn't make sense.
Keep something handy like a notepad or a pocketbook where you can write notes. Some artists have written songs in napkins. You never know when an idea will spark. So, keep a notebook with you at all times. Please keep your eyes open for ideas and write them down. One idea may form another opinion. It's like a chain reaction. Thoughts are precious and can take you to incredible places.
Look for creativity anywhere you go. It would help if you created that habit of recollection.
Make categories like those you'll find in this book, or create your categories.
Pro tip:
Carry a voice recorder.
Go for a walk and dictate what you are thinking.
Talk about it.
Use your senses.
Try to recollect memorabilia, photos, ephemera, write down interesting words, make up little poems, record your experiences, write down all of the songs you like. Make drawings.

- Keep several notebooks for each topic
- Record favorites. (Favorite quotes, meals, colors, etc.)
- Keep notes of your research and study
- Keep different tabs for each section.
- Keep it handy.
- Use post-its.
- Doodle
- Use samples of textures, fabrics, and colors
- Make your sketches and notes
- Internal Collecting
- External Collecting
- Memories
- Favorite Supplies

Lists

Lists are a great way to get you started in your creative journey, and this book is full of them! Create categories for each thing that you want to find out. Collect as many items as you can without doing research; when you can't come up with more items to add to your list, it is time to research the subject.

- Make lists of things that interest you.
- Name your projects
- Collect Interesting Words, the meaning, and the origin
- Collect quotes
- Make lists of something you don't know.
- Write 50 random objects.

Combining Ideas

Start by making two lists of related (or unrelated) items and place them side by side. Then, select one combination. Explore the relationship between these two elements. How are they similar or different? How can you create something with these two things?

Brainstorming

Brainstorming is a straightforward technique. Think of a word or a concept and write down everything you can think of for 20 minutes. So basically, the method is: sit down and think.

You'll find that the first few minutes are easy, but as you keep adding items to the list, it becomes increasingly difficult. It takes brainpower to do it, but we need to get used to it.

Just think and write all of those thoughts down. Make lists of everything you know about a specific topic you are interested in and keep them in your notebook. Do not discard anything. Even if you think your ideas are not related or seem crazy, it's useful to record them.

Try to be specific, like focusing on a word, phrase, or image. Immerse in the subject matter and do some research of the story or the idea.

Rules
- There are no bad ideas
- Respect all input
- Share the imperfect things
- Record every idea
- Be willing to be wrong
- Set time limits
- Keep going.

Challenges, pressure, and limits

Deadlines are motivators. Limits help with the creative process. In Apollo 13, an explosion occurred during the trip, and crew back on Earth worked with what they had to figure out a plan to bring back the team that was on board. They worked with a significant time constraint in a very high stakes scenario, and they eventually find a solution to the problem that made people return safely to Earth.

Fortunately, we don't have that kind of pressure when we are drawing, but if our life depended on coming up with new ideas, maybe we will do it all the time.

Prompts and challenges work for this reason. Setting limits works wonders for the brain.

You can use this book or any other book to set up a quick list. You can create your own prompt, too. There are tons of prompts on the internet to choose from, especially on Pinterest and blogs.

RULES

- Set a time limit: Examples: A 30-day challenge (where you draw something every day of that month)/ /Weekly/Daily/Every Sunday, etc.
- Source limits - Use only three colors.
- Use only three items from different lists.

Mindmapping

Mindmapping is a great technique to be creative. Mind mapping is making branching branches around a word, a combination of unrelated words or an idea. You can have a comment on the center or at the top of the page. Think about subtopics or things that remind you of that central word. You can also make questions like how, why, what, where, and when to explore the idea further.

It is exciting when we come up with new ideas. Mind maps can divide things into different sections and make them endless. Therefore this method is useful as a learning method.

Tony Buzan has some fantastic books that explain this process. He has some excellent examples that can help you visualize this in a better way

Questions

Asking questions is a primary method to come up with original ideas. Kids ask a lot of questions all the time to find out more about the world. On average, a kid will ask 125 questions in a day while adults only ask six questions. In a recent study about the role of creative questioning in the classroom, they find out that teachers ask questions to make the children think only 10% of the time in their class. We should encourage everyone to ask questions all the time, and artists should be no different.

Even though questions are simple, there are creative techniques that you can use to get to different types of answers. Sometimes we only need to ask the right question to find the obvious answer. Sometimes we need to ask the obvious questions to get a different answer.

Because art is an inherently creative activity, artists need to know how to make questions correctly. Think about all the ways that you can make your art different by just asking simple silly questions. Keep a notebook to write them all down.

I will suggest starting simple with these essential five questions, like Why, How, What, Where, When, and Who. Let's break them down.

What?

One of the most basic forms of questions. For example, What is a crocodile?" What do I want to do with the drawing? What can make it different?

How?

These types of questions can be elementary if you are doing research, like, for example, "How does a crocodile stay in the water?" or "How an alligator and a crocodile differ?" Or you can take it to other places like, "How can I make it different?" "How can I make this drawing different from other drawings?"

Why?

These types of questions work better with a problem. An example is the "five whys," a problem-solving method. Toyota, the car company, came up with this method to find solutions to their business problems. Ask a question about a problem that you have, and then ask why again to that answer, and you keep doing that until you find a solution.

Who, Where, and When?

You can research all of a crocodile's physical characteristics and habitats and ask things like: Where does a crocodile live? Or you can use this opportunity to take it to another level. Name the characters of the drawing and make up a little story.

CONCEPTUAL TECHNIQUES

Make intentional mistakes.

Try to doodle or write something and make it as awful as you can. It can be so liberating to do this. Try it.

TIPS:
Splatter some paint/coffee in your drawing.
Tear the page.
Use random colors.

Research a topic

As an artist, you need to explore the world and continuously learn new things. Curiosity is basic. Keep a notebook, especially for topics you don't know anything about but want to study. See who the current experts in the field are. Pretend you are one of the experts.

Metaphors and Analogies and The Myth

Writers use a lot of metaphors and analogies in their work. Collect them. It's a great way to communicate what you mean without saying it. It helps your brain to decipher things that are difficult to describe.

Get rid of the Cliché

A cliche is an overused phrase. First, we need to identify it. Keep an eye when you use clichés in your everyday life. Could you get rid of it or change it?

OTHER PRACTICAL TECHNIQUES

Start with you!

Individualize your ideas. Everyone has something to say, and everyone has different experiences in their lives, which makes us unique. Analyze what differences and similitudes you have with other people. Generally, we have very similar experiences with many people, but the way we interpret them can vary greatly.

Ask yourself questions and try to be the most honest. No one has to know the answers! Journal every day to learn more about what's on your mind.

Why do you like certain things better than others? Have you had any experience where you were the only one that like a particular thing in your friend's groups?

When you understand yourself better, you'll have more ideas for drawings and concepts because they will be meaningful.

Put yourself in everything that you create!
Ask yourself these questions:
What does your name mean?
What is your family's last name mean?
What do you like the most about yourself?
What do your parents have in common?
Customs and traditions in your family. What holidays do you celebrate and which ones you don't?
Things you like to do that makes you happy.
Things that you like to do in your free time

COLLECT LISTS OF FAVORITES

Favorite things change all the time, but it is good to keep lists of things you enjoy in your idea notebook. I have a list of things that I enjoy drawing, plans of things that I know about myself, and lists about my current favorite artists. Don't be shy to add items that are embarrassing or guilty pleasures!

1. Favorite song
2. Favorite food
3. Favorite color
4. Least Favorite song
5. Least Favorite food
6. Least Favorite color
7. Favorite time of day
8. Favorite animal
9. Favorite place
10. Favorite month
11. Favorite time of day
12. Favorite dessert
13. Favorite App
14. Favorite Artist
15. Favorite Quote
16. Favorite TV Show
17. Favorite movie
18. Favorite type of music
19. Favorite flower
20. Favorite tree
21. Favorite season
22. Favorite planet
23. Favorite superhero
24. Favorite month
25. Favorite pastime
26. Favorite puzzle
27. Favorite game
28. Favorite unpopular opinion
29. Favorite fruit
30. Favorite flavor
31. Favorite perfume

Take it a step further! Here are more techniques to explore:

- Describe yourself in an unfamiliar way. If you were another person, how would you see yourself?

- Write poems and short stories. Try making a mini poem with words that you have collected. Make up a short story or a flash fiction story to come up with a beginning, a middle, and an end.

- Record your commute. Keep notes of what you see in your way to work. Use your five senses.

- Personal Corkboard. Gather images that inspire you and attach them to a corkboard. They can be photos from different artists, post-it notes with ideas, or your sketches and illustrations. Place the corkboard somewhere in your office or your workplace where you can see it all the time; this will provide you with inspiration and motivation. From time to time, feel free to edit your items. You can keep adding items or get rid of things that are no longer interest you.

- Use Words. Make a list of words you find interesting. Research their origins and their meaning. Make a list of related stories. Try to use words that stimulate your creativity flow. Examples: Good words: Like, Love, Make, Happen, Build. Example of Bad words: Try, maybe, should, could, sort of, not sure.

- Write clues to solve something. Explore answers to unanswered or challenging questions.

- Write a lie in your journal. Tell lies in your journal, make up fake stories.

- Read a Classic Book or a movie. Take notes of the things you liked and the things you didn't like.
- Read about a famous historical event. Research the prominent people involved and do a timeline. Where does this information?
- Read Creativity Books and Art Books – Various books can help you with this.
- Do a menial and repetitive task. Sometimes when I'm at work, I have the best ideas. My work is very mechanical and repetitive, and at this point, I know the drill, so I tend to do it fast. Well, let me tell you, I have so many ideas when I'm there. I have post-its notes lying around at my office to use when I think about something for my drawings.
- Go to Sleep. Get a pocket notebook and place it permanently on your nightstand. That way, you don't have to go all the way where you keep your sketchbook.
- Use Coloring Books or take on other artistic projects. Take the pressure off by doing something unrelated to your art passion. If you are an oil painter, try watercolor. If you usually draw with a pen, try making clay sculptures. If you only draw black and white, paint a coloring book to think about the color palette you're going to use.
- Create new ideas for an everyday object. Think about ten things you can do with an item that it's not their real purpose. Use three unrelated things and come up with a list of things where you can use them.
- Talk in Gibberish. One player tells his or her partner about what happened that day in gibberish. The last person repeats the story in English.

- Use your non-dominant hand. Close your eyes, paint with your non-dominant hand, paint only with your hands, no tools.
- Habits. Make new habits, and break habits. Change the rules.
- Set a time limit. Say you are doing a project for one month.
- Don't take yourself too seriously. Play with dolls, make a mess, dance for no reason, etc.
- Motivational and Stimulation. Go to museums and galleries. Keep notes.
- Freewriting 3 pages. (The Artist's Way by Julia Cameron) Every day when you get up, write three pages of freewriting. Write everything that comes to your mind.
- Keep an idea place where your muses gather and throw ideas at you. For me, it's my idea notebook.

FINAL TIPS

Surround yourself with creative people.

Get in a class or a course where you'll find people that love art like you; this will stimulate your brain to think outside the box. Human beings are social beings, so we thrive when we are with like-minded people. Sharing ideas with someone is an excellent way to generate even more ideas.

Ask for advice.

There is nothing wrong with asking for advice. Search artists that you look up to and ask them questions about how they find ideas or how they keep being creative in their lives.

Curate your social media.

Adapt your social media to your liking. It will help you get more ideas because you're feeding yourself good content. Tell the algorithm with things you'd like to see in your feed. You do this by selecting posts from your favorite artists or those you find exciting and "liking and commenting" on those posts to engage with the creator. It's an excellent way to find people that like what you like.

Chapter 3

List of Projects

Projects will make you focus on one thing with a theme in common. They are fun to make. After you're done with the project, share what you've done.

Rules for developing a project:

- Set the Rules of the project!
- Create a Mood board for a project.
- Set a time limit
- Give it special meaning: It's helpful to think that someday your project will be in the hands of someone else. So make your project special. It can be meaningful for you only too!
- Visualize your project before starting.

Here are some examples for projects: you can take it a step further and document every step.

- Work on your Art Portfolio: Make 10 Illustrations for your portfolio. Keep the same style and concept throughout.
- Make a Daily Art Journal Page for a month.
- Make a series of Illustrations with the same Concept or Theme.
- Design a Character, name him/her, and write a mini short story for him/her.
- Fill two pages of your sketchbook with the same theme and use three colors. Ex: Horses/Baby Dinosaurs/Running, etc.
- Use old magazines or old books, cutouts, or ephemera to do art journaling.

- Design a photo album from your most recent trip.
- Make a mini-comic book. Basic bookbinding with one signature. Alternative. Make a mini-zine from a regular notebook page. (8 pages).
- Create a New Challenge or Follow a current challenge in social media. Example: The monthly character design challenge. (Characterdesignreferences.com)
- Draw a sticker set. Use five things from the same concept.
- Draw Your Day. What happened today? What are you feeling today?
- Make a 24- hour Comic Book. (an idea originally from Scott McCloud) It's a 24-page comic book written, drawn, and completed in 24 hours.
- Plan a Coloring Book –Make 15 - 20 Illustrations.
- Plan a children's book illustration – Use a 32-page book layout.
- Plan a music album. Come up with a concept and design.
- Write a Funny 4-panel Comic (Also called gag cartoon)
- Write a funny anecdote and make an illustration representing the anecdote. It could be the most embarrassing thing that has ever happened to you. Make an illustration that goes along with it.
- Write a poetry book.
- Write the premise of a superhero movie. One liner or script the first scene or the whole thing!
- Write a Personal Essay
- Write flash fiction.
- Write jokes for a stand-up routine or write something funny for a blog. Here's a prompt: explain your job to an alien.

- Read Classical Books from the Classic Book List (Chapter 13)
- Read about a historical event and make a timeline. Draw the main characters involved.
- Read about a country and make a map with icons for important cities/parks/etc.
- Create an illustration of a magazine article (Editorial Illustration)
- Watch a movie and draw the storyboard from a movie
- Color Study of a Movie Scene.
- Make a photo album.
- Make Paper Dolls out of Scrapbook /Pattern paper
- Make a mind map or brainstorm a project.
- Make five illustrations of a classic book or fairytale.
- Write a poem or a Song using classic themes like love, breakups, motivation, injustice, etc
- Write a song for kids.
- Create a Book Cover for a Classic book or a book you like
- Paint or Fix an old T-shirt.
- Plan a photograph session, choose a theme
- Take a photo of yourself and make a vector illustration out of it. Use bright colors.
- Make a pattern design for a fabric line in illustrator.
- Create a mythological character and give it a story.
- Look for art trends and style you like, list them in your notebook.
- Change something classic. Reinvent a logo for a well-known restaurant or coffee shop (example: Starbucks). How would you change the ending of a famous movie? Could you write it down or make a little comic?

Chapter 4
Tools for the visual artists

Even tools or supplies can be a great way to think about ideas. For example, you can take a tool and create a mind map around it where you ask yourself what is the best way to use it, or what new techniques can I learn from it?

Artist Concepts Toolbox:

Value
Form
Balance
Frame
Contrast
Composition
Perspective
Line Weight
Big, Medium and Small

Tools of the Trade:

Materials you'll going to need:
Pencil
Sharpener
Eraser
Paper
Water color Paint
Acrylic Paint
Brushes
Markers
Color pencils
Crayons
Digital Art

TYPES OF DRAWINGS /VISUAL ART MEDIUMS

1. Doodle and scribbles
2. Stick figures
3. Realistic Drawings
4. Realistic Portraits
5. Photorealism
6. Concept Illustrations
7. Character Design
8. Environment Design
9. Children's Books Illustrations
10. Editorial Illustrations
11. Spot illustrations
12. Flat illustrations
13. Comic books /Graphic Novel drawings
14. Cartoons and animation
15. 3-D modeling
16. Vector images
17. Typography /Calligraphy
18. Book Cover Illustrations
19. Scientific illustrations
20. Architecture
21. Urban Sketching
22. Graffiti
23. Art Journal
24. Pencil Drawing
25. Colored pencil art
26. Oil Painting
27. Acrylic Painting
28. Watercolour/Gouache Painting
29. Pastel Painting
30. Charcoal Painting
31. Storyboarding

Chapter 5
People

Portraits and Full Bodies

One of the main things we want to draw is ourselves. Art is our expression of us as human beings interacting with this world. No wonder we want to learn how to draw our faces and bodies first. Some people say that portraits are the most challenging thing to draw, and when you do it right, people will be surprised. We need to look for our loved ones from the crowd. That's why when we see a portrait, we immediately notice when something's off.

The portrait of a person is the best way to learn how to draw the different parts of the face. Images of someone's face are essential; that is why kings wanted their picture made; it was their way of telling the world that they were different and unique. We also see this in the Hollywood industry, where actors take headshots. When you start doing portraits, you can also use your face, or of those from celebrities, so you immediately can see if the resemblance is good. Use magazines and photos to practice in your sketchbook.

Another essential in an artist's armamentarium is learning to draw the full figure. The different poses and gestures make a person unique. Poses standing, sitting, walking, talking, and running are different in each person. It is best to observe a person in real life; for example, you can go to a restaurant, draw someone there or take a figure drawing class.

TYPES OF RELATIONSHIPS

1. Portrait. Facial features
2. Full Body
3. Adult
4. Children
5. Toddler
6. New Born Baby
7. Tweens Kids
8. Teenager
9. Young Adult
10. Elderly
11. Best friends.
12. Parent
13. Parens and Children
14. Romantic Couple
15. Three
16. Four
17. Groups of 5
18. Family
19. Friends
20. Enemies
21. Lovers
22. Client and Service Provider
23. Boss and Employer
24. Hero vs Villain
25. Office coworkers
26. Hero and friends
27. Hero and sidekick
28. Classmates
29. Teacher and student
30. Doctor and nurse
31. Doctor and patient

BASIC EMOTIONS

Our emotions affect our entire bodies, but especially our faces. Our face contains many muscles that work pushing and pulling a group to convey a different feeling. Our communication depends on them. That's how we can tell the emotional state of another person; sometimes, we call it a "vibe."

In the character design process, the artist always draws the character in six or more different emotions without losing its prominent features.

The Resting face: The BASIC face without muscles contracting.
Happy: Smiling and eyes shrinking.
Angry: Eyebrows are essential here.
Confused: Eyebrows in different directions.
Sad: Eyebrows upward, corner of the mouth downward.
Mischievous: One corner of the mouth smiling.
Skeptical: Eyelids half-open.
Surprised: Eyebrows up and mouth opened.
Excited: Eyebrows up but mouth open and smiling.
Scared: Show the white of the eye.

OCCUPATIONS

Most likely, it's that for your creative projects; you will need a character. And that character needs a job. So, I made these lists to provide you some ideas for different kinds of jobs.
The first list is people with regular jobs, from an airline pilot to a housewife. The second list is supernatural or fantastic occupations like superheroes or vampires.
You can make up occupations and keep adding to these lists. You can also create an ideal job of your own or a fantasy job. Try to come up with different styles for each job.

Examples: What if you need five types of doctors characters?

LIST OF OCCUPATIONS

1. Housewife
2. Airline Dispatcher
3. Airline Pilot
4. Flight Attendant
5. Business
6. Accountant
7. Administrative Assistant/Secretary
8. Advertising
9. Consultant
10. Financial Advisor
11. Insurance Agent
12. Investment Banker
13. Doctor
14. Nurse
15. Paramedic
16. Psychologist
17. Social Worker
18. Veterinarian
19. Military Careers
20. Police Officer
21. Teacher
22. Bank teller
23. Call center
24. Cook / Chef
25. Hair stylist
26. Personal Fitness Trainer
27. Retail
28. Sales
29. Ski Instructor
30. Waiter
31. Wedding Planner
32. Computer Programmer
33. Actor
34. Architect
35. Art Appraiser

36. Art Auctioneer
37. Artist
38. Museums Curator
39. Music Conductor
40. Musician
41. Librarian
42. Freelance Editor
43. Writer
44. Editor
45. Sport Player
46. Tennis Player
47. Golf Player
48. Runner
49. Soldier
50. President
51. Queen
52. King
53. Football Player
54. Basketball Player
55. Photographer
56. Chemist
57. Engineer
58. CEO
59. Laboratorist
60. Physicist

FAMOUS CHARACTERS FROM WORLD HISTORY

1. Martin Luther
2. Alexander the Great
3. Plato
4. Aristoteles
5. Christopher Columbus
6. Napoleon Bonaparte
7. Neil Armstrong
8. George Washington
9. Charlemagne
10. William the Conqueror
11. Genghis Khan
12. Babur
13. Kublai Khan
14. Ferdinand and Isabella
15. Shi Huangdi
16. Sakagawea
17. Alfred the Great of England
18. Brian Boru
19. Julius Caesar
20. Nobunaga Oda
21. Marco Polo
22. Ieyasu Tokugawa
23. Joan of Arc
24. James VI of Scotland
25. Frederick the Great
26. George Washington
27. Nelson Mandela
28. Simon Bolivar
29. Shulgi
30. Cleopatra
31. Attila the Hun

TYPES OF PERSONALITY TRAITS

1. Joyful
2. Greedy
3. Optimist
4. Quiet
5. Diplomat
6. Idealist
7. Bold
8. Imaginative
9. Strong-willed
10. Good nature
11. Leaders
12. Innovative
13. Analysts
14. Charming
15. Explorer
16. Attractive
17. Relaxed
18. Gentle
19. Careful
20. Daring
21. Witty
22. Modest
23. Selfish
24. Gullible
25. Ignorant
26. Deceitful
27. Silly
28. Moody
29. Helpful
30. Decisive
31. Practical

MYTHOLOGY CHARACTERS

1. Aphrodite
2. Apollo
3. Ares
4. Artemis
5. Athena
6. Demeter
7. Dionysus
8. Hephaestus
9. Hera
10. Hermes
11. Hestia
12. Poseidon
13. Zeus
14. Achilles
15. Adonis
16. Circe
17. Cyclopes
18. Atlas
19. Cronus
20. Agave
21. Cerberus
22. Calypso
23. Centaur
24. Eros
25. Hades
26. Icarus
27. Gaea
28. Medusa
29. Narcissus
30. Minotaur
31. Prometheus

FANTASTIC FAMOUS CHARACTERS

1. Historical Common Person (Ancient greek, Ancient Rome, Ancient Egypt)
2. Mermaid
3. Fairy
4. Vampire
5. Comic Superhero
6. Comic Villain
7. Comic Sidekick
8. King
9. Queen
10. Princess
11. Knights
12. Warriors
13. Peasant
14. Ninja and Samurai
15. Pirates
16. Witch
17. Frankenstein (Character)
18. Monster
19. Mummy
20. Angel
21. Robot
22. Objects: Car, Airplane
23. Werewolf
24. Ghost
25. Medusa
26. Devil
27. Ogre
28. Goblin
29. Trolls
30. Sprite
31. Werwolf

POSES AND GESTURE

When we first start learning how to draw, it's natural that our drawing will look kind of stiff and without personality. We rarely see a person just standing there, doing nothing and looking forward; it's weird when we do. That's why it's good to learn poses and gestures. It will change your drawings when you add an exciting pose. Giving your characters a pose it's an opportunity to tell a story.

The key to a right pose lies in a design principle, which is balance. A person may be "just standing there," but the body would always try to find a balance, so we move our hips to one side, cross our arms, grab our pockets or our hips.

Live references like a figure drawing class it's the best way to get better at this. Here is a list of some of the classic possess.

1. Standing
2. Sitting
3. Walking
4. Running
5. Jogging
6. Jumping
7. Fighting
8. Dancing
9. Flying
10. Spinning
11. Kneeling
12. Punching
13. Crawling
14. Climbing
15. Lifting
16. Sleeping
17. Crouching
18. Lying down
19. Twisting

Two people:
20. Talking
21. Staring
22. Kissing
23. Choking
24. Fighting
25. Slapping

Weapons
26. Shooting
27. Blasts
28. Bow
29. Guns
30. Nunchucks
31. Staff
32. Swords
33. Knife42. Walking
43. Wall and ball
40. Street sports
41. Strength sports
42. Walking
44. Aquatic and paddle sports

With Props

34. Walking with a cane
35. Carrying an umbrella
36. Carrying a bag
37. Putting makeup on
38. Driving a car
39. Eating
40. Drinking
41. Smoking
42. Talking on the phon
43. Wearing a cape
44. Getting dressed

With animals:

45. Walking the dogs
46. Playing with cat
47. Riding a horse
48. Using a Fishing rod

SPORTS

One of the easiest things to give your character personality is to make them do an activity like a sport. You can think of so many sports; I would suggest you pick and choose the one that you love but also ones that you don't have any idea what they are about so you can create something new and exciting and maybe learn something new.

1. Yoga
2. Pilates
3. Aerobics
4. Dancing
5. Archery
6. Soccer
7. Football
8. Baseball
9. Basketball
10. Hockey
11. Ice Skating
12. Tennis
13. Swimming
14. Marathon Runners
15. Climbing
16. Cycling
17. Combat sports
18. Baton twirling
19. Cue sports
20. Dog sports
21. Equestrian sports
22. Fishing
23. Golf
24. Handball
25. Hunting
26. Ice sports
27. Kite sports
28. Parkour
29. Racket sports
30. Rodeo originated
31. Running
32. Sailing
33. Snow sports
34. Shooting sports
35. Stacking
36. Stick and ball games
37. Hockey
38. Lacrosse
39. Polo
45. Canoeing
46. Kayaking
47. Rafting
48. Rowing
49. Competitive swimming
50. Weightlifting
51. Motorized sports
52. Auto racing
53. Motorboat racing
54. Motorcycle racing
55. Card games
56. E-sports
57. Strategy board games
58. Air sports
59. Athletics (track and field)
60. Electronic sports
61. Endurance sports
62. Target sport

Chapter 6
Animals

We love animals, and we love to draw them. There are hundreds of thousands of animals you can choose to start drawing. Below, I give you a list of some of the world's animal categories.

MAMMALS

1. Opossums
2. Numbat
3. Koala
4. Wombats
5. Brushtail Possums or Cuscuses
6. Pygmy possums
7. Honey Possums or Noolbenger
8. Bettongs
9. Wallabies
10. Kangaroos
11. Tasmanian Devil
12. Marsupial Lions
13. Diprotodon
14. Anteaters
15. Sloths
16. Armadillos
17. Lemurs
18. Lorises
19. Marmosets
20. Tamarins
21. Capuchins
22. Squirrel Monkey
23. Night or owl monkees
24. Titis
25. Sakis
26. Uakaris
27. Howler
28. Spider monkey
29. Woolly Spider
30. Wooly monkeys
31. Baboons
32. Macaques
33. Gibbons
34. Orangutans
35. Gorillas
36. Chimpanzees
37. Humans (See People, for examples)
38. Pangolins
39. Asian Black bear
40. American Black bear
41. Brown bear
42. Giant Panda
43. Polar Bear
44. Sun bear
45. Sloth bear
46. Spectacled bear
47. Raccoons
48. Red Panda
49. Weasels
50. Badgers
51. Otters
52. Ferrets
53. Martens
54. Minks
55. Wolverines
56. Red Pandas
57. Skunks
59. Canidae
60. Wolves
61. Coyote
62. Dogs
63. Foxes
64. Otters
65. Skunks
66. Seals
67. Walrus
68. Earless seals
69. Sea lions
70. Fur seals

71. Earless seals
72. Lion
73. Tigers
74. Leopard
75. Snow Leopard
76. Small Wild Cats
77. Cheetahs
78. Domestic Cats
79. Mongooses
80. Civets
81. Hyaenas
82. Treeshrews
83. Glires
84. Mice
85. Rats
86. Chipmunks
87. Squirrels
88. Guinea pigs
89. Hamsters
90. Capybara
91. Gerbils
92. Voles
93. Praire dogs
94. Groundhogs
95. Chinchillas
96. Mountain Beavers
97. New World Flying Squirrels
98. Beavers
99. Porcupines
100. Kangaroo rats
101. Pocket Gophers
102. Deer mice
103. True mice
104. Birch mice
105. Jumping mice
106. Pygmy jerboas
107. Rabbit
108. Hares
109. Pikas
110. Hedgehogs
111. Moonrats
112. Shrews
113. Desmans
114. Moles
115. Solenodons
116. Aardvark
117. Elephants
118. Manatees
119. Hyraxes
120. Tapirs
121. Rhinos
122. Horses
123. Zebras
124. Donkeys
125. Camels
126. Llamas
127. Alpaca
128. Guanaco
129. Vicuña
130. Pigs
131. Peccaries
132. Pygmy hog
133. Giant forest hog
134. Bushpig
135. Red River hog
136. Warthhog
137. Babirusa
138. Banteng
139. Gaur
140. Gayal
141. Eruopean Bison
142. American bison
143. Wild yak
144. Yak
145. Zebu

146. Domestic Cattle
147. Buffalo
148. Water Buffalo
149. Antelopes
150. Sheep
151. Goats
152. Muskoxen
153. Deer
154. Muntjac
155. Elk
156. Red Deer
157. Fallow Deer
158. Chital
159. Reindeer
160. Roe deer
161. Mule deer
162. Moose.
163. Musk deer
164. Giraffe
165. Okapi
166. Pronghorn
167. Hippos
168. Baleen whale
169. Rorquals
170. Right whale
171. Bowhead wheal
172. Toothed whale
173. Pygmy right whale
174. Gray whale
175. Dolphins
176. Porpoises
177. Belugas
178. Narwhals
179. River Dolphins
180. Sperm whales : Moby Dick
181. Beaked whale

REPTILES AND AMPHIBIANS

1. Turtle
2. Sea turtles
3. Crocodile
4. Alligator
5. Gavials
6. Snakes
7. Wart
8. American pipe
9. Dwarf pipe
10. Stiletto
11. Boas
12. Mauritius
13. Colubrids
14. Asian pipe
15. Elapids
16. Python
17. Dwarf boas
18. Shield-Tailed Snakes
19. Vipers
20. Worm Lizards
21. Agamas
22. Chameleon
23. Iguanas
24. Geckos
25. Tuatara
26. Dinosaurs
27. Caecilians
28. Salamanders
29. Newts
30. Mudpuppies
31. Frogs
32. Toads

FISH

1. Anglerfish
2. Armorhead
3. Bass
4. Bat ray
5. Betta
6. Billfish
7. Blackfin Tuna
8. Blowfish
9. Blue Shark
10. Boafish
11. Brill
12. Capelin
13. Carp
14. Catfish
15. Clown fish
16. Clown loach
17. Cornetfish
18. Crappies
19. Discus
20. Dory
21. Eagle ray
22. Electric ray
23. European eel
24. Flagfin
25. Flounder
26. Frogfish
27. Glowlight danio
28. Goldfish
29. Koi
30. Mahi-mahi
31. Lionfish

BIRDS

1. Ostriches
2. Rhea
3. Cassowary
4. Emus
5. Kiwi
6. Tinamous
7. Moa
8. Chickens
9. Ducks
10. Nightjars
11. Ollibirds
12. Potoos
13. Frogmouth
14. Apodiformes
15. Turacos
16. Bustards
17. Cuckoos
18. Pigeons
19. Mesites
20. Sandgrous
21. Rails
22. Cranes
23. Flamingos
24. Grebes
25. Waders
26. Tropicbirds
27. Sunbitterns
28. Kagu
29. Albatross
30. Petrels
31. Penguins
32. Storks
33. Boobies
34. Cormorants
35. Pelicans
36. Herons
37. Egrets
38. Hoatzin
39. New World Vultures
40. Hawks
41. Eagles
42. Owls
43. Cuckoo roller
44. Trogons
45. Quetzals
46. Hornbills
47. Falcons
48. Parrots
49. Seriemas
50. Passerines
51. Toucans

INSECTS

1. Jumping Bristletails
2. Silverfish
3. Firebrat
4. Bees
5. Wasps
6. Ants
7. Beetles
8. Cockroaches
9. Termites
10. Flies
11. Mayflies
12. Dragonflies
13. Stoneflies
14. Webspinners
15. Rockcrawlers
16. Earwigs
17. Mantises
18. Stick insects
19. Crickets
20. Grasshoppers
21. Angel insects
22. Booklice
23. Lice
24. Thrips
25. Cicadas
26. Aphids
27. Snakeflies
28. Alderflies
29. Dobsonflies
30. Fish flies
31. Lacewings

CRUSTACEANS AND ARTHROPODES

1. Brine Shrimp
2. Fairy Shrimp
3. Water Fleas
4. Tadpole Shrimp
5. Clam Shrimp
6. Horseshoe shrimp
7. Ramipedia
8. Bernacles
9. Copepods
10. Seed Shrimp
11. Crabs
12. Lobsters
13. Shrimp
14. Crayfish
15. Krill
16. Mantis Shrimp
17. Woodlice
18. Hooded shrimp
19. Scuds
20. Sandhopper
21. Pauropoda
22. Millipedes
23. Centipedes
24. Symphyla
25. Arthropleuridea
26. Spiders
27. Scorpions
28. Mites
29. Ticks
30. Sea scorpions: Extinct
31. Horseshoe crabs

MOLLUSCS AND OTHER ANIMALS

1. Sea spiders
2. Caudofoveata
3. Slugs
4. Polyplacophora
5. Chitons
6. Monoplacophora
7. Gastropoda
8. Snails
9. Cephalopoda
10. Squid
11. Octopus
12. Cuttlefish
13. Nautilus
14. Spirula
15. Cockles
16. Clams
17. Oysters
18. Scallops
19. Geoducks
20. Mussels
21. Scaphopoda
22. Tusk shells
23. Corals
24. Actiniaria
25. Vampire Squid
26. Sea anemones
27. Zoanthids
28. Blue-ringed octopus
29. Cirrina
30. Sponges
31. Jellyfish

LEGENDARY ANIMALS

1. Dragons
2. Cipactli
3. Unicorns
4. Pegasus
5. Alicorns
6. Chimera
7. Bigfoot
8. Merlion
9. Yeti, Abominable Snow Man
10. Minotaur
11. Cyclops
12. Centaur
13. Lochness monster
14. Sphinx
15. Hydra
16. Harpies
17. Cerberus
18. Apis Bull
19. Nandi
20. Kelpie
21. Anansi
22. Double-headed monster
23. Phoenix
24. Gremlin
25. Gargoyle
26. Leviathan
27. Vodyanoy
28. World-elephants
29. Ceffyl Dŵr
30. Gullinkambi
31. Kraken

Chapter 7
Nature

FLOWERING PLANTS

1. Moschatel
2. Sweetgum
3. Cashew
4. Dogbane
5. Holly
6. Ivy
7. Birch
8. Trumpet Creeper
9. Cactus
10. Cannabis
11. Dogwood
12. Dipterocarpaceae
13. Ebenaceae
14. Heath
15. Eucommia
16. Pea
17. Beech
18. Boojum
19. Witch-hazel
20. Walnut
21. Laurel
22. Paradise nut
23. Mallow
24. Mahogany
25. Mulberry
26. Myrtle
27. Souther Beech
28. Tupelo
29. Olive
30. Paulowonia
31. Plane
32. Mangrove
33. Rose
34. Bedstraw
35. Rue
36. Willow
37. Sapindaeae (Soapberry)
38. Sapodilla
39. Simaurobaceae
40. Camellia
41. Thymelaea
42. Elm
43. Verbeneceae
44. Agavaceae
45. Palm
46. Laxmanniaceae
47. Poaceae
48. Ruscaceae
49. Annonaceae (Custard apple)
50. Lauraceae (Laurel Family)
51. Magnolia
52. Nutmeg

FRUITS

1.	Apples	30.	Elderberry
2.	Bananas	31.	Feijoa
3.	Berries	32.	Fig
4.	Açaí	33.	Goji berry
5.	Apple	34.	Gooseberry
6.	Akee	35.	Grape
7.	Apricot	36.	Raisin
8.	Avocado	37.	Grapefruit
9.	Banana	38.	Guava
10.	Bilberry	39.	Honeyberry
11.	Blackberry	40.	Huckleberry
12.	Blackcurrant	41.	Jabuticaba
13.	Black sapote	42.	Jackfruit
14.	Blueberry	43.	Jambul
15.	Boysenberry	44.	Japanese plum
16.	Buddha's hand	45.	Jostaberry
17.	Crab apples	46.	Jujube
18.	Currant	47.	Juniper berry
19.	Cherry	48.	Kiwano (horned melon)
20.	Cherimoya (Custard Apple)	49.	Kiwifruit
21.	Chico fruit	50.	Kumquat
22.	Cloudberry	51.	Lemon
23.	Coconut	52.	Lime
24.	Cranberry	53.	Loquat
25.	Cucumber	54.	Longan
26.	Damson	55.	Lychee
27.	Date	56.	Mango
28.	Dragonfruit (or Pitaya)	57.	Mangosteen
29.	Durian	58.	Marionberry
30.	Elderberry	59.	Melon
		60.	Cantaloupe

61.	Honeydew	90.	Rambutan (or Mamin Chino)
62.	Watermelon	91.	Redcurrant
63.	Miracle fruit	92.	Salal berry
64.	Mulberry	93.	Salak
65.	Nectarine	94.	Satsuma
66.	Nance	95.	Soursop
67.	Olive	96.	Star apple
68.	Orange	97.	Star fruit
69.	Blood orange	98.	Strawberry
70.	Clementine	99.	Surinam cherry
71.	Mandarine	100.	Tamarillo
72.	Tangerine	101.	Tamarind
73.	Papaya	102.	Ugli fruit
74.	Passionfruit	103.	White currant
75.	Peach	104.	White sapote
76.	Pear	105.	Yuzu
77.	Persimmon		
78.	Plantain		
79.	Plum		
80.	Prune (dried plum)		
81.	Pineapple		
82.	Pineberry		
83.	Plumcot (or Pluot)		
84.	Pomegranate		
85.	Pomelo		
86.	Purple mangosteen		
87.	Quince		
88.	Raspberry		
89.	Salmonberry		

VEGETABLES

1. Amaranth
2. Arugula
3. Beet
4. Borage
5. Brocooli
6. Brussels Sprouts
7. Cabbage
8. Catsear
9. Celtic
10. Chaya
11. Chickweed
12. Chicory
13. Chinese mallow
14. Chrysathemum
15. Collard greens
16. Common purslane
17. Corn salad
18. Dandelion
19. Dill
20. Endive
21. Fat hen
22. Fiddlehead
23. Fluted pumpkin
24. Turnip
25. Radish
26. Carrot
27. Parsnip
28. Beetroot
29. Lettuce
30. Beans
31. Broad beans
32. Kuka
33. Komatsuma
34. Lagos bologi
35. Lamb's lettuce
36. Lamb's quarters
37. Land crees
38. Peas
39. Potato
40. Eggplant
41. Tomato
42. Cucuber
43. Pumpkin /Squash
44. Onion
45. Orache
46. Pak Choy
47. Pea
48. Radicchio
49. Rapini
50. Sea kale
51. Garlic
52. Leek
53. Pepper
54. Spinach
55. Yam
56. Sweet potato
57. Cassava
58. Beans and subtypes
59. Stem Vegetables
60. Root and tuberous vegetables

FLOWERS

1. Aconite
2. Ageratum
3. Allium
4. Anemone
5. Angelica
6. Angelonia
7. Artemisia
8. Aster
9. Astilbe
10. Aubrieta
11. Azalea
12. Balloon Flowers
13. Balsam
14. Baneberry
15. Basket of Gold
16. Bee Balm
17. Begonia
18. Bellflowers
19. Bergenia
20. Blackeyed
21. Bleeding Heart
22. Bloodroot
23. Boneset
24. Browalia
25. Bugleweed
26. Bugloss
27. Buttercup
28. Butterfly Weed
29. Caladium
30. Calendula
31. California Poppy
32. Canterbury Bells
33. Cardinal Flower
34. Carnation
35. Castor Bean
36. Catmint
37. Celosia
38. Chives
39. Chrysanthemum
40. Clary Sage
41. Cleome
42. Coleus
43. Columbine
44. Comfrey
45. Cornflower
46. Coreopsis
47. Corydalis
48. Cosmos
49. Crocus
50. Crown Imperial
51. Cushion Spurge
52. Cyclamen
53. Daffodill
54. Dahlia
55. Daisy
56. Dame's Rocket
57. Delphinium
58. Diascia
59. Dusty Miller
60. Dutchman's Breeches

61.	Epimedium	91.	Leadwort
62.	Evergreen Candytuft	92.	Lemon Balm
63.	Fennel	93.	Lily
64.	Fountain Grass	94.	Lobelia
65.	Foxglove	95.	Lupine
66.	Gaillardia	96.	Maiden Pink
67.	Gas Plant	97.	Malva
68.	Gaura	98.	Marigold
69.	Gazania	99.	Mirabilis
70.	Geranium	100.	Moonflower
71.	Geum	101.	Morning Glory
72.	Gobe Thistle	102.	Nastartium
73.	Glory of the Snow	103.	Nierembergia
74.	Goatsbeard	104.	Orchid
75.	Golden Marguerite	105.	Osteospermum
76.	Gomphrena	106.	Pansy
77.	Heliotrope		Pearly Everlasting
78.	Hepatica	107.	Perennial Flax
79.	Hollyhock	108.	Periwinkle
80.	Hosta	109.	Petunia
81.	Hyacinth	110.	Pincushion
82.	Hyssop	111.	Polka Dot Plant
83.	Impatiens	112.	Primrose
84.	Iris	113.	Ranunculus
85.	Jack in the Pulpit	114.	Red Valerian
86.	Jacob's Ladder	115.	Rock Soapwort
87.	Lady's Mantle	116.	Rose
88.	Lantana	117.	Rue
89.	Lavender	118.	Sanvitalia
90.	Lavender Cotton	119.	Scarlet Sage

120. Sea Lavender
121. Sea Thrift
122. Shirley Poppy
123. Shooting Star
124. Silvermound
125. Skunk Cabbage
126. Snapdragon
127. Snow in Summer
128. Snowdrop
129. Solomon's Seal
130. Spring Snowflake
131. Summer Slavory
132. Sunflower
133. Sweet Alyssum
134. Sweet Woodruff
135. Tansy
136. Thunbergia
137. Tithonia
138. Torenia
139. Trillium
140. Tulip
141. Verbena
142. Violet
143. Virginia Bluebell
144. Wild Senna
145. Windflower
146. Yarrow
147. Yellow Archangel
148. Yellow Loosestrife
149. Zinnia

NATURAL PHENOMENON

1. Rainbow
2. Clouds
3. Rain
4. Drizzle
5. Cloudburst
6. Deluge
7. Downfall
8. Downpour
9. Rainfall
10. Rainstorm
11. Storm
12. Pour
13. Precipitate
14. Storm
15. Sunlight
16. Full Moon
17. Haze
18. Tornado
19. Hurricane
20. Tsunami
21. Waterfall
22. Sunrise
23. Sunset
24. Monsoon
25. Mizzle
26. Smoke
27. Nightime
28. Dusk
29. Lava (Volcano Eruption)
30. Flood
31. Dawn

RIVERS

1. Amazon
2. Amu Darya
3. Amur
4. Apalachicola
5. Arkansas
6. Arno
7. Atchafalaya
8. Baltic-White Sea Canal
9. Black Warrior
10. Brahmaputra
11. Cape Cod Canal
12. Cape Fear
13. Chao Phraya
14. Chattahoochee
15. Chesapeake and Delaware Canal
16. Colorado
17. Columbia
18. Congo (Zaire)
19. Connecticut
20. Cumberland
21. Danube (Donau)
22. Delaware
23. Dnieper
24. Dniester
25. Don (Tanais)
26. Douro (Duero)
27. Elbe
28. Erie Cana
29. Euphrates
30. Ganges (Ganga)
31. Garonne
32. Grand Canal (Da Yunhe)
33. Green
34. Guadalquivir
35. Houston Ship Channel
36. Hudson
37. Illinois Waterway
38. Indus
39. Intracoastal Waterway
40. Irrawaddy
41. Irtysh River
42. James
43. Jordan
44. Kanawha
45. Kasai
46. Kentucky
47. Kiel Canal
48. Kwai
49. Lena
50. Liffey
51. Limpopo (Crocodile)
52. Loire
53. Mackenzie
54. Madeira
55. Marne
56. Mekong
57. Mississippi
58. Missouri
59. Mobile
60. Monongahela

61. Moscow Canal
62. Murray-Darling
63. Nelson
64. New York State Barge Canal
65. Niagara
66. Niger
67. Nile
68. Ob River
69. Oder
70. Ohio
71. Orange
72. Orinoco
73. Ouachita
74. Panama Canal
75. Paraguay
76. Paraná
77. Pará-Tocantins
78. Plata
79. Po
80. Potomac
81. Purus
82. Red
83. Rhine
84. Rhine-Main-Danube Waterway
85. Rhone
86. Rio Grande (Rio Bravo)
87. Roanoke
88. Sacramento
89. Saint Johns
90. St. Lawrence
91. Salween
92. San Joaquin
93. Sao Francisco
94. Sault Ste. Marie Canals
95. Savannah
96. Seine
97. Shannon
98. Shatt-al-Arab
99. Snake
100. Somme
101. Suez Canal
102. Syr Darya
103. Tagus
104. Tennessee
105. Tennessee-Tombigbee Waterway
106. Thames
107. Tiber
108. Tigris
109. Tombigbee
110. Tunguska, Lower
111. Ural
112. Vistula
113. Volga
114. Volga-Baltic Canal
115. Volga-Don Canal
116. Welland Canal
117. Willamette
118. Yangtze
119. Yazoo
120. Yellow (Huang He)
121. Yenisei
122. Yukon
123. Zambezi

MOUNTAIN RANGES

1. Adirondacks
2. Altai Shan
3. Ahaggar
4. Alaska Range
5. Aleutian Range
6. Alps
7. Andes
8. Apennines
9. Appalachians
10. Ararat
11. Athos, Mt
12. Atlas Mts
13. Balkan Mountains
14. Barisan Mts
15. Black Hills
16. Brooks Range
17. Cantabrian Mts
18. Carpathian Mts
19. Cascade Range
20. Caucasus Mts
21. Cerro Chirripo
22. Cévennes
23. Coast Mts
24. Coast Ranges
25. Daxue Shan
26. Drakensberg Range
27. Elburz (Alborz) Mts
28. Ellsworth Mts
29. Fujiyama
30. Ghats, Western
31. Great Dividing Range
32. Guiana Highlands
33. Harz Mts
34. Himalayas
35. Hindu Kush
36. Jotunheimen
37. Jura Mts
38. Karakoram
39. Kenya
40. Kilimanjaro
41. Kunlun Shan
42. Laurentian Mts
43. Mackenzie Mts
44. Mauna Kea
45. Mauna Loa
46. Olympus, Mt
47. Ouachita Mts
48. Ozarks
49. Pamirs
50. Parnassus, Mt
51. Pegunungan Maoke
52. Pennines
53. Pikes Peak
54. Pindus Mts
55. Pisgah
56. Pontic Mts
57. Pyrenees
58. Queen Maud Mts
59. Rhodope Mts
60. Rocky Mts

61. Ruwenzori
62. San Bernardino Mts
63. San Gabriel Mts
64. Sayan Mts
65. Sierra Madre Occidental
66. Sierra Madre del Sur
67. Sierra Maestra
68. Sierra Nevada
69. Sierra Nevada, Spain
70. Sinai, Mt
71. Soback-san
72. Southern Alps
73. Sulaiman Range
74. Taeback-san
75. Taurus Mts
76. Tian Shan
77. Tibesti Mts
78. Transantarctic Mts
79. Ural Mts
80. Virunga Mts
81. Vosges Mts
82. Washington, Mt
83. Wind Rinver Range
84. Wind River Range
85. Wrangell Mts
86. Zagros Mts

ELEMENTS OF THE EARTH

1	H	Hydrogen	31	Ga	Gallium
2	He	Helium	32	Ge	Germanium
3	Li	Lithium	33	As	Arsenic
4	Be	Beryllium	34	Se	Selenium
5	B	Boron	35	Br	Bromine
6	C	Carbon	36	Kr	Krypton
7	N	Nitrogen	37	Rb	Rubidium
8	O	Oxygen	38	Sr	Strontium
9	F	Fluorine	39	Y	Yttrium
10	Ne	Neon	40	Zr	Zirconium
11	Na	Sodium	41	Nb	Niobium
12	Mg	Magnesium	42	Mo	Molybdenum
13	Al	Aluminum	43	Tc	Technetium
14	Si	Silicon	44	Ru	Ruthenium
15	P	Phosphorus	45	Rh	Rhodium
16	S	Sulfur	46	Pd	Palladium
17	Cl	Chlorine	47	Ag	Silver
18	Ar	Argon	48	Cd	Cadmium
19	K	Potassium	49	In	Indium
20	Ca	Calcium	50	Sn	Tin
21	Sc	Scandium	51	Sb	Antimony
22	Ti	Titanium	52	Te	Tellurium
23	V	Vanadium	53	I	Iodine
24	Cr	Chromium	54	Xe	Xenon
25	Mn	Manganese	55	Cs	Cesium
26	Fe	Iron	56	Ba	Barium
27	Co	Cobalt	57	La	Lanthanum
28	Ni	Nickel	58	Ce	Cerium
29	Cu	Copper	59	Pr	Praseodymium
30	Zn	Zinc	60	Nd	Neodymium

61	Pm	Promethium	91	Pa	Protactinium
62	Sm	Samarium	92	U	Uranium
63	Eu	Europium	93	Np	Neptunium
64	Gd	Gadolinium	94	Pu	Plutonium
65	Tb	Terbium	95	Am	Americium
66	Dy	Dysprosium	96	Cm	Curium
67	Ho	Holmium	97	Bk	Berkelium
68	Er	Erbium	98	Cf	Californium
69	Tm	Thulium	99	Es	Einsteinium
70	Yb	Ytterbium	100	Fm	Fermium
71	Lu	Lutetium	101	Md	Mendelevium
72	Hf	Hafnium	102	No	Nobelium
73	Ta	Tantalum	103	Lr	Lawrencium
74	W	Tungsten	104	Rf	Rutherfordium
75	Re	Rhenium	105	Db	Dubnium
76	Os	Osmium	106	Sg	Seaborgium
77	Ir	Iridium	107	Bh	Bohrium
78	Pt	Platinum	108	Hs	Hassium
79	Au	Gold	109	Mt	Meitnerium
80	Hg	Mercury	110	Ds	Darmstadtium
81	Tl	Thallium	111	Rg	Roentgenium
82	Pb	Lead	112	Cn	Copernicium
83	Bi	Bismuth	113	Nh	Nihonium
84	Po	Polonium	114	Fl	Flerovium
85	At	Astatine	115	Mc	Moscovium
86	Rn	Radon	116	Lv	Livermorium
87	Fr	Francium	117	Ts	Tennessine
88	Ra	Radium	118	Og	Oganesson
89	Ac	Actinium			
90	Th	Thorium			

GEMSTONES

1. Pride of Australia
2. Red Admiral Opal
3. Jade
4. Amber
5. Jet
6. Pearl
7. Arco Valley Pearl
8. La Peregrina
9. Satlada
10. Pearl of Lao Tzy
11. Pearl of Puerto
12. Turquoise
13. Hematite
14. Quartz
15. Malachite
16. Jasper
17. Rose
18. Amethyst
19. Moss Agate
20. Tigers-eye
21. Chrysocolla
22. Pyrite
23. Tourmaline
24. Diamonds
25. Diaria-i-Noor
26. DeYoung Red Diamond
27. Desden Green Diamond
28. Esperanza Diamond
29. Florentine Diamond
30. Great Mogul Diamond
31. Hope Diamond
32. Koh-i-Noor
33. Koi Diamond
34. Noor-ol-Ain Diamond
35. Oppenheimer Diamond
36. Orlove
37. Portuguese Diamond
38. Raven Diamond
39. Ragent Diamond
40. Sancy
41. Star of Sierra Leone
42. Star of the South
43. Tiffany Yellow Diamond
44. The Symbolic Yellow Diamond
45. Wittelsbach Graff Diamond
46. Aquamarines
47. Dom Pedro
48. Topaz
49. Spinels
50. Black Prince-s Ruby
51. Samarin Spinel
52. Timur Ruby
53. Alexandrites
54. Ruby
55. Emerald
56. Sapphire
57. Onyx
58. Lapis Lazuli
59. Opal

Chapter 8
Objects and Props

TYPES OF CLOTHES

1. Outerwear
2. Sweaters
3. Waistcoats
4. Jackets
5. Coats
6. Suits
7. Skirts
8. Dresses
9. Active wear
10. Social wear or special occasion wear
11. Leg wear
12. Neckwear
13. Evening wear
14. Uniforms and work wear
15. Knit wear
16. Sleep wear
17. Underwear
18. Accessories
19. Beachwear
20. Shoes

TOPS

1. Asymmetrical
2. Off shoulder
3. Batwing
4. Bralette
5. Boxy
6. Blouson
7. Body suit
8. Bustier
9. Camisole
10. Cape
11. Cardigans
12. Sweaters
13. Crop top
14. Cardigans
15. Sweaters
16. Choker
17. Corset
18. Collar
19. Cold-shouldered
20. Draped
21. Empire line
22. Flashdance
23. Halter
24. Henley
25. High Low
26. Kaftan
27. Keyhole
28. Lace up
29. Layered
30. Maxi
31. One shoulder
32. Peasant
33. Poncho
34. Peplum
35. Princess line
36. Raglan sleeve
37. Spaghetti strap
38. Sweatshirt
39. Swing
40. Shirt
41. Smoch
42. Shell
43. Tie front
44. Tube
45. Tupic
46. T-shirt
47. Wrap
48. X-ray
49. Yoke

DRESSES

1. Aline dress
2. Tent dress
3. Yoke dress
4. Empire line dress
5. Shift dress
6. Drindle dress
7. Sheath dress
8. Low or drop waist dress
9. Tunic dress
10. Princess seam dress
11. Blouson dress
12. Shirt waist dress
13. Wrap around dress
14. Peasant Dress
15. Baby doll dress
16. Body con dress
17. Cocktail dress
18. Debutante dress
19. Skater dress
20. Camisole dress
21. Pinafore dress /Jumber dress
22. Granny dress
23. Harem dress
24. Trumpet dress / Mermaid dress
25. Maxi dress
26. Apron dress
27. Sweater dress
28. Swing dress
29. Tutu dress
30. Sun Dress
31. Little Black Dress
32. Coat dress
33. Corset dress
34. Balloon Dress
35. Bouffant dress
36. Fit and flare dress
37. Handkerchief hem Dress
38. Gathered dress
39. Kaftan Dress
40. Pillowcase dress
41. Slip Dress
42. Shirt dress
43. Ball gown
44. Party dress
45. Strapless Dress

SKIRTS

1. A line skirt
2. Fitted skirt
3. Drindle skirt
4. Tiered skirt
5. Sarong drape Skirt
6. Layered skirt
7. Circle skirt
8. Gored skirt
9. Trumpet skirt
10. Wrap skirt
11. Divided skirt
12. Pleated skirt
13. Asymmetrical Hem skirt
14. Bubble Skirt
15. Yoke Skirt

PANTS

1. Straight pants
2. Jeans
3. Overalls or jumpsuits
4. Culottes
5. Harem pants
6. Baggy pants
7. Bell Bottoms
8. Tights or leggings
9. Punk Pants
10. Eastern pants
11. Jodhpur pants
12. Dungarees

SHORTS

1. Booty shorts
2. Boy shorts
3. Jamaican shorts
4. Bermuda shorts
5. Knee length shorts
6. Pedal pusher shorts
7. Toreador shorts
8. Capri
9. Boyfriend shorts
10. Chino shorts
11. Cut off shorts
12. Wrap shorts
13. Cargo Shorts
14. Slipshort
15. Skorts
16. Swimming trunk shorts
17. Boxer shorts
18. Board shorts

SHOES

1. Athletic Shoes
2. Beach shoes or water shoes
3. Boat shoes or Deck shoes
4. Ballet shoes, or ballet slipper
5. Ballet flat.
6. Pointe shoe
7. Bast shoe
8. Blucher shoe
9. Brogan (shoes) or Brogue shoe
10. Brothel creeper or creepers
11. Cantabrian albarcas
12. Chelsea boot or Dealer boots
13. Chopine
14. Climbing shoe
15. Clog, footwear made of wood
16. Court shoe or pump.
17. Cross country running shoe
18. Derby shoe or Gibson.
19. Diabetic shoe or extra depth
20. Dori shoes or Ballet boot
21. Dress shoe, for formal events.
22. Earth shoe
23. Elevator shoes
24. Espadrille
25. Fashion boot, for women
26. Figure skates or Ice skates
27. Flip-flops, a type of sandal.
28. Galesh, traditional footwear of Iran
29. Galoshes or gum shoes
30. Golf shoes

31. Giveh
32. High Heels
33. High-top, ankle length
34. Huarache
35. Inline Skates
36. Roller Skating
37. Jazz Shoe
38. Jelly Shoes
39. Jump boots
40. Jutti
41. Kitten Heel
42. Kolhapuri Chappal
43. Kung Fu shoe
44. Loafers or Slip-ons
45. Mary Jane or Doll Shoes.
46. Mojari
47. Moccasin
48. Monk shoe or monk strap
49. Mule, a shoe with no back
50. Opanak
51. Opinga
52. Pointinini
53. Rocker bottom shoe
54. Ruby slippers
55. Russian boot
56. Saddle shoe or saddle oxford
57. Sandal, open type footwear
58. Silver Shoes
59. Slip-on shoe
60. Slipper

BAGS

1. Purse
2. Athletic Bags
3. Backpack
4. Backpack purse
5. Barrel Bag
6. Baguette Bag
7. Basket Bag
8. Bowling Bag
9. Bucket Bag
10. Clutch Bag
11. Cosmetic Case
12. Clutch
13. Doctor's Bag
14. Duffle Bag
15. Envelope Bag
16. Feed Bag
17. Fold over clutch
18. Hobo Bag
19. Messenger Bag
20. Minaudiere
21. Muff
22. Pouch Bag
23. Quited Bag
24. Saddlebag
25. Satchel
26. Shoulder Bag
27. Tote Bag
28. Wristlet

CLOTHING ACCESSORIES

1. Hats
2. Belts
3. Handbags
4. Shoes
5. Gloves
6. Muffs
7. Necklaces
8. Socks
9. Scarves
10. Shawls
11. Eyewear
12. Hand fans
13. Parasols
14. Umbrellas
15. Wallets
16. Glasses
17. Bonnets
18. Stockings
19. Ceremonial Swords
20. Canes
21. Sashes
22. Lanyards
23. Piercings
24. Ties
25. Bonnets
26. Suspenders
27. Watches
28. Umbrellas
29. Parasols
30. Fans

JEWELRY

1. Chains
2. Rings
3. Bracelets
4. Pendants
5. Necklaces
6. Choker
7. Gold
8. Diadem
9. Earrings
10. Ear cuffs
11. Hatpin
12. Hairpin
13. Tiara
14. Belly chain
15. Brooch
16. Anklet
17. Toe ring
18. Crown
19. Bangle
20. Locket
21. Anklet
22. Breastplate
23. Cuff links
24. Championship ring
25. Engagement ring
26. Toe ring
27. Wedding ring
28. Amulet
29. Rosary beads
30. Membership pin

KITCHEN

1.	Cookware	31.	Roaster with Rack
2.	Saute Pan	32.	Oval Roaster
3.	Sauce Pan	33.	Wok
4.	Sauce Pan with Lid	34.	Cooling Rack
5.	Fry Pan	35.	Storage Set
6.	Pan with Lid	36.	Teapots and Teakettles
7.	Soup Pot with Lid	37.	Kettle
8.	Double Boiler	38.	Tea Kettle
9.	Stockpot	39.	Gooseneck Kettle
10.	Skillet	40.	Richmond
11.	Cream Grill Pan	41.	Le Creuset
12.	Round Gril Pan	42.	Breville
13.	Panini Press	43.	Teapot
14.	Oval Au Gratin Dish	44.	Tea Press
15.	Deep Skillet		
16.	Everyday Pans		
17.	White Baking Dish		
18.	Melting Pot		
19.	Oval Dutch Oven		
20.	Paella Pan		
21.	Pizza Pans		
22.	Baking Dish		
23.	Cookie Sheet		
24.	Bakeware Set		
25.	Pie Dish		
26.	Quiche Dish		
27.	Mini Ramekin		
28.	Au Gratin Dish		
29.	Ramekin		
30.	Round Cocotte		

Kitchen Accessories

1. Storage Jars
2. Cream and Sugar set
3. Coffee Storage Jars
4. Ren Canister
5. Squeezer
6. Thermal Carafe
7. Coffe Grinder
8. Travel Mugs
9. Coffee Filters
10. Baking Utensils
11. Cooking Utensils
12. Brass plating
13. Spoon
14. Slotted Spoon
15. Ladle
16. Turner
17. Slotted Turner

BATHROOM

1. Toilet
2. Toilet paper
3. Toilet paper
4. Toothbrush
5. Towels
6. Canisters
7. Plunger
8. Tissue Box
9. Shower
10. Shower Curtain
11. Shower Curtain liner
12. Soap dispensers
13. Wire baskets
14. Totes
15. Trash can
16. Carafe
17. Mirror
18. Trash can
19. Bath Towels
20. Bath Rugs
21. Curtains
22. Bath mirrors
23. Bath mat
24. Toothbrush holder
25. Storage cart
26. Storage Containers
27. Drawer trays
28. Hamper
29. Room Spray
30. Rubber Gloves
31. Candles

BEDROOM

1. Headboard
2. Footboard
3. Mattress frame
4. Mattress
5. Box spring
6. Mattress pad
7. Sheets
8. Pillowcases
9. Bed
10. Bedskirt
11. Sleeping pillows
12. Specialty pillows
13. Blankets
14. Chair
15. Lamps
16. Desk
17. Rugs
18. Ottoman
19. Bookends
20. Dressers
21. Clothing
22. Closet
23. Writing desk
24. Vanity table
25. Artwork
26. Posters
27. Prints
28. Candles
29. Candleholders
30. Vases
31. Television Stand

TYPES OF FOODS

1. Appetizers
2. Condiments
3. Confectionery
4. Convenience
5. Desserts
6. Dried Foods
7. Dips
8. Fermented
9. Fast food
10. Noodles
11. Pies
12. Salads
13. Sandwiches
14. Snack
15. Soups
16. Stews
17. Legumes
18. Edible plants
19. Edible fungi
20. Edible nuts and seeds
21. Baked goods
22. Dairy products
23. Eggs
24. Meat
25. Cereals
26. Seafood
27. Staple foods
28. Candy

PIES, PUDDING AND TARTS

1. Apple pie
2. Blackberry pie
3. Blueberry pie
4. Cherry pie
5. Bumbleberry pie
6. Grape pie
7. Key lime pie
8. Mince pie
9. Strawberry pie
10. Strawberry rhubarb pie
11. Fruit Puddings
12. Malvern pudding
13. Mango pudding
14. Ozark pudding
15. Persimmon pudding
16. Summer pudding
17. Banana Cream Pie
18. Caramel tart
19. Pască
20. Coconut Cream pie
21. Jamaican patty
22. Karelian pasties
23. Key lime pie
24. Knish
25. Lemon ice box pie
26. Pear tart
27. Pecan pie
28. Quiche
29. Raspberry pie
30. Walnut piet
31. Flan

MUSIC INSTRUMENTS

1. Accordion
2. Accordiola
3. Air horn
4. Alboka
5. Alphorn
6. Alto horn
7. Arghul
8. Atenteben
9. Bagpipe
10. Balaban
11. Bansuri
12. Baritone Horn
13. Bassoon
14. Violin
15. Cello
16. Double bass
17. Fiddle
18. Gusle
19. Lirone
20. Octobass
21. Viola
22. Vielle
23. Dutar
24. Harp
25. Chapey
26. Cak
27. Cuk
28. Huobosi
29. Mandolin
30. Guitar
31. Charango
32. Piano
33. Agung a Tamlang
34. Bamboo slit drum
35. Balafon
36. Cajon
37. Castanets
38. Clapsticks / Clave sticks
39. Cymbal
40. Glockenspiel
41. Handpan/Hang Drum
42. Marimba
43. Mbira
44. Steelpan
45. Triangle
46. Vibraphone
47. Wood Block
48. Xylophone
49. Membranophone
50. Agida
51. Alcahuete
52. Apinti
53. Arobapa
54. Ashiko
55. Assotor
56. Baboula
57. Balaban
58. Balsie
59. Bamboula
60. Bari

61.	Barrel drum	91.	Maktoum
62.	Barriles	92.	Mridangam
63.	Bass Drum	93.	Naqara
64.	Bodhran	94.	O-daiko
65.	Bongo drums	95.	Okedo-daiko
66.	Boobam	96.	Octaban
67.	Candombe	97.	Pakhavaj
68.	Chenda	98.	Pandero
69.	Conga	99.	Piccolo Snare
70.	Cuica	100.	Sabar
71.	Dabakan	101.	Samphor
72.	Daf	102.	Shime-jishi-daiko
Davul		103.	Snare
73.	Dhaa	104.	Surdo
74.	Dimdi	105.	Tabla
75.	Dholak	106.	Taiko
76.	Dhol	107.	Talking drum
77.	Dollu	108.	Timpani
78.	Dunun		
79.	Drum kit		
80.	Gran Cassa		
81.	Hira-daiko		
82.	Illimbia drum		
83.	Ingomba		
84.	Janggu		
85.	Kakko		
86.	Kanjira		
87.	Kendang		
88.	Lambdeg drum		
89.	Madhalam		
90.	Madal		

TECHNOLOGY

1. Computers
2. Cables
3. Batteries
4. Cameras
5. Cellphones
6. Smartphones
7. Television
8. Radio
9. USB Stick
10. Memory Card
11. Headphones
12. Printer
13. Laptop
14. Router
15. Webcam
16. Microphone
17. Diskette
18. MP3 Player
19. Electric Fan
20. Electric drill
21. Speakers
22. Vacuum Cleaner
22. Blender
23. Coffee machine
24. Iron
25. Hair dryer
26. Washing machine
27. Dryer machine
28. Video games consoles
29. Meat Grinder
30. Rice Cooker
31. Refrigerator

TRANSPORTATION

1. Car
2. Microcar
3. Hatchbacks
4. City car
5. Supermini
6. Family car
7. Sedan
8. Crossover SUV
9. Minivans-MPVs
10. Luxury vehicle
11. Sports cars
12. Hot hatch
13. Grand tourer
14. Supercar
15. Muscle car
16. Convertible
17. Van
18. Bi-articulated bus
19. Coaches
20. Customized buses
21. Double-decker
22. Electric buses
23. Fuel cell buses
24. Full -size buses
25. Green buses
26. Half-cab buses
27. Intercity
28. Low-entry buses
29. Low-floor buses
30. Midibuses
31. Minibuses
32. Open-top buses
33. School buses
34. Single-deck buses
35. Steam buses
36. Step-entrance buses
37. Tri-axle buses
38. Trolleybuses

BICYCLES AND MOTORCYCLES

39. Motorcycles
40. Cruiser
41. Chopper
42. Honda gold Wing motorcycle
43. Scooter
44. Step-through motorcycle
45. Conventional street motorcycle
46. Sport bike
47. Touring motorcycle
48. Sport touring motorcycle
49. Standard motorcycle
50. Underbones
51. Mopeds
52. Off-road motorcycle
53. Enclosed motorcycle
54. Tricycles
55. Road Bicycle
56. Touring Bicycle
57. Randonneur Bicycle
58. Hybrid Bicycle
59. Flat bar Bicycle
60. Cyclo-cross
61. Utility Bicycle
62. Freight Bicycle
63. Ice Bicycle
64. Mountain Bicycle
65. Military Bicycle
66. Tacing Bicycle
67. Time trial Bicycle
68. Triathlon Bicycle
69. Track Bicycle
70. BMX Bicycle
71. Cruiser Bicycle
72. Motorized Bicycle
73. Gyroscopic Bicycle
74. Electric Bicycle
75. Railbikes
76. Firefighter Bicycle

TRAINS AND AIRCRAFTS

77. Long-distance trains
78. High-speed train
79. Inter-city train
80. Regional train
81. Higher-speed train
82. Short distance trains
83. Commuter train
84. Heavy rail train
85. Metro train
86. Subway train
87. Tube train
88. Underground train
89. Tram train
90. Light rail
91. Monorail
92. Maglev train
93. Railcar train
94. Civil aircraft
95. Research, prototypes and specials aircraft
96. Military aircraft
97. Seaplanes
98. Amphibians aircraft
99. Flying Boats
100. Single-Engine Piston
101. Business Jet aircraft
102. Tricycle Gear
103. Amphibians
104. Taildraggers
105. Helicopter
106. Tiltrotor
107. Light-sport aircraft
108. Turboprop
109. Powered parachute
110. Ultralights aircraft
111. Multiengine piston
112. Light Sport Aircraft
113. Floatplanes or Seaplanes
114. Biplanes
115. Airbus
116. Gliders
117. Gyroplanes
118. Kitbuilts or Homebuilts
119. Powered Parachutes
120. Airships (blimps and Dirigibles)

BOATS AND SUBMARINES

121. Balloons
122. Airboat
123. Banana boat
124. Barge
125. Bass boat
126. Boita
127. Bow rider
128. Bracera
129. Cabin cruiser
130. Cruise ship
131. Cable ferry
132. Canoe
133. Cape Islander
134. Captain's gig
135. Car-boat
136. Car float
137. Catamaran
138. Center console
139. Coble
140. Coracle
141. Cornish pilot gig
142. Crash rescue boat
143. Cuddy boat
144. Cutter
145. Dhow
146. Dhoni
147. Dinghy
148. Dory
149. Dredging
150. Dragon boat
151. Drift boat
152. Drifter
153. Dugout
154. Durham boat
155. Electric boat
156. Express cruiser
157. Faering
158. Ferry
159. Fireboat
160. Fishing boat
161. Float tube
162. Flyak
163. Flying boat
164. Folding boat
165. Friendship boat
166. Full rigged
167. Garbage scow
168. Go-fast
169. Gondola
170. Gundalow
171. Great Lakes
172. houseboat
173. Hovercraft
174. Hydrofoil
175. Higgins
176. Hydroplane
177. Ice boat
178. Inflatable boat
179. Jetboat
180. jet ski

181. Jon boat
182. Jukung
183. Junk
184. Kayak
185. Keelboat
186. Ketch
187. Kettuvallam
188. Launch
189. Landing craft
190. lifeboat
191. Lighter
192. LNG carrier
193. Log boat
194. Langschiff
195. Longboat
196. Longship
197. Longtail
198. Lugger
199. Luxury yacht
200. Machinaw boat
201. Masula boat
202. Missile boat
203. Monitor
204. Motorboat
205. Motor Launch
206. Narrowboat
207. Nordland
208. Norfolk
209. Optimist
210. Outrigger
211. Padded-V
212. Paddle streamer
213. Patrol boat
214. pedalo
215. Personal water craft
216. Pinnace
217. Pink
218. Pirogue
219. Pleasure barge
220. Pleasure craft

278. Attack submarines
279. Ballistic missile
280. Guided Missile submarine
281. Deep Submergence Rescue submarine
282. Cruise missile submarines

Chapter 9
PLACES

COUNTRIES

1. Africa
2. Algeria
3. Democratic Republic of the Congo
4. Sudan
5. Libya
6. Chad
7. Niger
8. Angola
9. Mali
10. South Africa
11. Ethiopia
12. Mauritania
13. Egypt[a]
14. Tanzania
15. Nigeria
16. Namibia
17. Mozambique
18. Zambia
19. Morocco
20. South Sudan
21. Somalia
22. Central African Republic
23. Madagascar
24. Botswana
25. Kenya
26. Cameroon
27. Zimbabwe
28. Republic of the Congo
29. Ivory Coast (Côte d'Ivoire)
30. Burkina Faso
31. Gabon
32. Guinea
33. Ghana
34. Uganda
35. Senegal
36. Tunisia
37. Malawi
38. Eritrea
39. Benin
40. Liberia
41. Sierra Leone
42. Togo
43. Guinea-Bissau
44. Lesotho
45. Equatorial Guinea
46. Burundi
47. Rwanda
48. Djibouti
49. Eswatini (Swaziland)
50. Gambia, The
51. Cape Verde
52. Comoros
53. Mauritius
54. São Tomé and Príncipe
55. Seychelles
56. North America
57. Antigua and Barbuda
58. Barbados
59. Belize
60. Canada

61.	Costa Rica	91.	Uruguay
62.	Cuba	92.	Suriname
63.	Dominica	93.	Asia
64.	Dominican Republic	94.	Afghanistan
65.	El Salvador	95.	Armenia
66.	Grenada	96.	Azerbaijan*
67.	Guatemala	97.	Bahrain
68.	Haiti	98.	Bangladesh
69.	Honduras	99.	Bhutan
70.	Jamaica	100.	Brunei
71.	Mexico	101.	Cambodia
72.	Nicaragua	102.	China
73.	Panama	103.	Cyprus
74.	Saint Kitts and Nevis	104.	Georgia*
75.	Saint Lucia	105.	India
76.	Saint Vincent and the Grenadines	106.	Indonesia*
77.	The Bahamas	107.	Iran
78.	Trinidad and Tobago	108.	Iraq
79.	United States	109.	Israel
80.	South America	110.	Japan
81.	Brazil	111.	Jordan
82.	Argentina	112.	Kazakhstan*
83.	Peru	113.	Kuwait
84.	Colombia	114.	Kyrgyzstan
85.	Bolivia	115.	Laos
86.	Venezuela	116.	Lebanon
87.	Chile	117.	Malaysia
88.	Paraguay	118.	Maldives
89.	Ecuador	119.	Mongolia
90.	Guyana	120.	Myanmar

121.	Nepal	151.	Belgium
122.	North Korea	152.	Bosnia and Herzegovina
123.	Oman	153.	Bulgaria
124.	Pakistan	154.	Croatia
125.	Palestine	155.	Cyprus
126.	Philippines	156.	Czechia
127.	Qatar	157.	Denmark*
128.	Russia*	158.	Estonia
129.	Saudi Arabia	159.	Finland
130.	Singapore	160.	France*
131.	South Korea	161.	Georgia*
132.	Sri Lanka	162.	Germany
133.	Syria	163.	Greece
134.	Taiwan	164.	Hungary
135.	Tajikistan	165.	Iceland
136.	Thailand	166.	Ireland
137.	Timor-Leste	167.	Italy
138.	Turkey*	168.	Kazakhstan*
139.	Turkmenistan	169.	Kosovo
140.	United Arab Emirates	170.	Latvia
141.	Uzbekistan	171.	Liechtenstein
142.	Vietnam	172.	Lithuania
143.	Yemen	173.	Luxembourg
144.	Europe	174.	Malta
145.	Albania	175.	Moldova
146.	Andorra	176.	Monaco
147.	Armenia*	177.	Montenegro
148.	Austria	178.	Netherlands*
149.	Azerbaijan*	179.	North Macedonia
150.	Belarus	180.	Norway

181. Poland
182. Portugal
183. Romania
184. Russia*
185. San Marino
186. Serbia
187. Slovakia
188. Slovenia
189. Spain*
190. Sweden
191. Switzerland
192. Turkey*
193. Ukraine
194. United Kingdom*
195. Vatican City
196. Oceania - Australia
197. Australia
198. Federated States of Micronesia
199. Fiji
200. Indonesia*
201. Kiribati
202. Marshall Islands
203. Nauru
204. New Zealand
205. Palau
206. Papua New Guinea
207. Samoa
208. Solomon Islands
209. Tonga
210. Tuvalu
211. United States of America (Hawaii)
212. Vanuatu
213. Antartica

PLACES

1. City
2. Road
3. Avenue
4. Street
5. Highway
6. Roundabout
7. Freeway
8. Bank
9. Community Center
10. Motel
11. Elevator
12. Gas Station
13. Library
14. Morgue
15. Park
16. Police Station
17. Buildings
18. Houses
19. Hospital
20. Diner
21. Amusement Park
22. Circus
23. Nightclub
24. Rock Concert
25. Zoo
26. Supermarket
27. General Store
28. Restaurants
29. Bars
30. Hospital
31. Office building
32. Swimming Pool
33. Farm
34. Castle
35. Gym
36. Coffee House
37. School
38. Bodies of water
39. Swamp
40. River
41. Lake
42. Sea
43. Ocean
44. Desert
45. Beach
46. Jungle
47. Forest
48. Mountain Top
49. Tundra
50. Sky
51. Underwater
52. Space
53. Other Planet
54. Sun
55. Galaxy

Chapter 10
THEME CHALLENGES

I believe the more you know of a subject, the more you can have ideas. And, it doesn't hurt to know a little more, I mean, you never know. I always research random things because I'm curious about how things work. I make notes on my monthly idea notebook, and as usual, I draw them.

A theme is a great way to come up with new ideas. It can make everything cohesive and aesthetically pleasing. Use it for when you're working on your art portfolio. Or create a project choosing only one article of a theme.

In this chapter, these are some of the ideas you'll find: sticker sets, greeting cards, toys, candies, and gifts.

Seasons

Events

Party

Weddings

Christmas

Travel

Back to School

Sea

Love and Romance

Symbols

Zodiac Signs

WINTER

1. Snow
2. Snowflakes
3. Ice Skates
4. Sweater
5. Scarves
6. Hats
7. Gloves
8. Boots
9. Ice
10. Coats
11. Snowman
12. Freezing
13. Glacial
14. Frosty
15. Polar
16. Arctic
17. North
18. Siberian
19. Hibernal
20. Boreal
21. Frozen lakes
22. Frozen
23. Cloudy
24. Shrammed
25. Nither
26. Gelid
27. Overcast
28. Frozen lake
29. Transparent
30. Icy
31. Pale

SPRING

1. Flowers
2. Birds
3. Easter Hunt
4. Rabbit
5. Pasture
6. Blue Sky
7. Basket
8. Sundresses
9. Picnic
10. April Showers
11. Spring break
12. Carnival
13. Lent
14. Flowering plants
15. Blooming
16. Warmth
17. Hail
18. High winds
19. Temperate
20. Rebirth
21. Mardi Gras
22. Saint Patrick's Day
23. Resurrection
24. Passover
25. Butterfly
26. Pink
27. Pastel Colors
28. Easter Bunny
29. Chicks
30. Flower Bloom
31. May Day

SUMMER

1. Palm trees
2. Sun tan
3. Bathing suits
4. Hot
5. Beach
6. Vacations
7. Hotel Resort
8. Beach View
9. Sea
10. Waves
11. Surfboards
12. Snorkling
13. Hawaii
14. Swimming
15. Sunglasses
16. Beach Towel
17. Bright Sunlight
18. Bathing Suit
19. Pool
20. Pool float
21. Flip Flops
22. Sun hat
23. Watermelon
24. Lemonade
25. Flamingo
26. Orange
27. Cast Shadows
28. Bright Colors
29. Watermelon
30. Fruity Drunks
31. Cancun

AUTUMN

1. Gold Leaf
2. Pumpkin
3. Thanksgiving
4. Halloween
5. Cold weather
6. Scarves
7. Sweaters
8. High Boots
9. Cozy
10. Trees change color
11. Trees shed their leaves
12. Leaves on the ground
13. Harvest
14. Fall
15. Melancholia
16. Back To School
17. American football season
18. Metal
19. White Tiger of the West
20. Golden Brown
21. Orange
22. Brown
23. Red leaves
24. Apples
25. Melancholia
26. Pumpkin Pie
27. Autumn Foliage
28. Grey sky
29. Labor Day
30. Golden
31. Coats

EVENTS, CELEBRATIONS AND HOLIDAYS

Holidays and special days are a great way to create something cohesive. Of course, there are so many holidays in this world that it could be impossible to name them all. I give you some of the best known holidays in the USA but feel free to add your own. Keep a calendar to keep track of the most important holidays so you can prepare ahead of time. For example, the last quarter of the year is one of the most crucial times for business. November and December are months that are very busy with holidays, so art sales are up. Illustrators and other artists prepare for this time of year.

10 HOLIDAYS MOST COMMONLY CELEBRATED IN THE US
1. Christmas Day
2. Thanksgiving
3. Mother's Day
4. Easter
5. Independence Day (Fourth of July)
6. Father's Day
7. Halloween
8. Valentine's Day
9. St Patrick's Day
10. New Year's Day (New Year's Eve)

PARTY

1. Happy
2. Cakes
3. Cupcakes
4. Thematic Party
5. Happy Music
6. Costume Party
7. Get Together
8. Reunions
9. Decorations
10. Salon – Event Rooms
11. Party planner
12. Catering
13. Wine
14. Toast
15. Dinner
16. People
17. Invitations
18. Conversation
19. Small Talk
20. Formal dress
21. Fancy china
22. Photos
23. Group Photos
24. Balloons
25. Gifts
26. Joyous occasion
27. Celebration
28. Guests
29. Winning Game
30. Team Celebrations
31. Birthdays

WEDDINGS

1. Bride
2. Groom
3. Something borrowed
4. Something blue
5. Wedding Guests
6. Bridesmaids
7. Toast
8. Wedding Reception
9. Wedding Cake
10. Wedding Dress
11. Veil
12. Vows
13. Church
14. Pastor/Judge/rabi/
15. Family and in -laws
16. Gala
17. Dancing
18. Celebration
19. Invitations
20. Love
21. Small Talk
22. Conversation
23. Bridal Shower
24. Flower arrangement
25. Guest sitting
26. Wedding planner
27. Dinner
28. Photos
29. Wedding rings
30. Flower Bouquet
31. Invitations

CHRISTMAS

1. Gingerbread Man Cookies
2. Santa Claus
3. Gingerbread House
4. Christmas Tree
5. North Pole
6. Ice Skating
7. Christmas Tree Ornaments
8. Jingle Bells
9. Ugly Sweater
10. Hot Cocoa
11. Gifts
12. Christmas Eve Dinner
13. Stockings
14. Rudolph the Red Nose Reindeer
15. Frosty the Snowman
16. A Christmas Carol
17. Peppermint
18. Ponsietta
19. Advent Calendar
20. Nativity Scene
21. Three Wise Men
22. Ribbons
23. Wreaths
24. Candles
25. Garlands
26. Mistletoe
27. Knitted Sweater
28. Fireplace
29. Christmas lights
30. Christmas Swags
31. Polar Bear

TRAVEL

1. Hotel
2. Tourist
3. Architectural Landmarks
4. Tickets
5. Passports
6. Beach Resorts
7. Roadtrip
8. Airports
9. Compass
10. Bags / Suitcases
11. Baggage Claim
12. Camera
13. Postcard
14. Maps
15. Compass
16. Camera Photos
17. Postcards
18. Souvenirs
19. Business trip
20. Sandals
21. Bikini
22. Tote Bag
23. Train Station
24. Beach towels
25. Cocktails
26. Sunglasses
27. Night clubs
28. Travel log
29. Vacations
30. Receipts
31. Downtown

BACK TO SCHOOL

1. School
2. Pencils
3. Bulletin board
4. School bus
5. Crayola box
6. Classroom
7. Teacher
8. Students
9. Backpack
10. Notebooks
11. Textbooks
12. Blackboard
13. Homework
14. Ruler
15. Calculator
16. Spelling
17. Highlighters
18. Index cards
19. Sharpie pens
20. Ballpoints pens
21. Eraser
22. Calendar
23. Printer
24. Lunch bags
25. Binder
26. Gym Bag
27. New Sneakers
28. Locker
29. Pencil pouch
30. Glue stick
31. Folders

SEA

1. Oceans
2. Seven seas
3. Neptune
4. Seafood
5. Sailor
6. Captain
7. Pirate
8. Lifeguard
9. Rafting
10. Fishing
11. Swimming
12. Sailing
13. Whale
14. Moby Dick
15. Anchor
16. Boat
17. Pirate Ship
18. Boat rope
19. Sailor knots
20. Lighthouse
21. Captain wheel
22. Ancient ship
23. Nautical
24. Stripes
25. Sailor cap
26. Fish
27. Compass
28. Boat's Lifeguard
29. Pelican
30. Seahorse
31. Octopus

LOVE AND ROMANCE

1. Hearts
2. Cupid
3. Love
4. Kisses
5. Gifts
6. Chocolate Box
7. Date
8. Hugs
9. Romantic Dinner
10. Candles
11. Single Red Rose
12. Photos
13. Love Greeting Cards
14. Gift giving
15. Dating
16. Romantic dinners
17. Candy
18. Passion
19. Valentine's Day
20. Blind Date
21. Love Letters
22. Chocolate Strawberry
23. XOXO
24. Double Date
25. Wedding
26. Heart Lollipops
27. Heart Sugar Cookies
28. Conversation Hearts
29. Romantic Comedies
30. Holding Hands
31. Bouquet of Red Roses

SYMBOLS

1. Flags
2. Cup
3. Crown
4. Shadow
5. Valley
6. Mask
7. 4 Elements
8. Rainbow
9. Triangle
10. Circle
11. Square
12. The One
13. Star
14. Mirror
15. Sun
16. Moon
17. Heart
18. Throne
19. Labyrinth
20. Fruit
21. Victory
22. Sword
23. Stairs
24. North
25. Dance
26. Eagle
27. Tree
28. Twins
29. Tiger
30. Mother

THE 12 ZODIAC SIGNS

1. Aries
2. Taurus
3. Gemini
4. Cancer
5. Leo
6. Virgo
7. Libra
8. Scorpio
9. Sagittarius
10. Capricorn
11. Aquarius
12. Pisces

THE 12 CHINESE ZODIAC SIGNS

1. Rat
2. Ox
3. Tiger
4. Rabbit
5. Dragon
6. Snake
7. Horse
8. Sheep
9. Monkey
10. Rooster
11. Dog
12. Pig

Chapter 11
Colors

Colors of colors: Colors have a different meaning in different parts of the world, and artists use them in various contexts. This list gives you a general idea of what colors mean in art.

Black: Black has been the color of solemnity and authority. Example: Worn by judges.
White: Purity. Innocence. Example: The bride wears a white wedding dress.
Yellow: Greatness, humor, spontaneity. Example: Taxicabs are commonly yellow.
Red: Red is the color of courage and sacrifice. Also, of danger and passion. Example: Red is the primary color of Valentine's day.
Orange: The color of extroverts, energy, and unconventional. Example: The color of life jackets.
Green: Associated with nature and health. Example:
Blue: Means intelligence, confidence, harmony. Example: Sailors wear blue.
Purple: The color of royalty and magic. Example: Worn by monarchs.

Popular Color Combinations

- Black and white
- Red and blue
- Yellow and Blue:
- Green, Red and white
- Black and Blue
- Orange and Green
- Yellow and Orange
- Blue and Gray
- Red and White
- Blue and White
- Blue and Purple

COLORS

1. Chartreuse
2. Spring Green
3. True Green
4. Burnt Ochre
5. Lime peel
6. Olive Green
7. Grass Green
8. Lilac
9. Yellow Green
10. Poppy Red
11. Carmine Red
12. Magenta
13. Tuscan Red
14. Peach
15. Blush Pink
16. Light peach
17. Carnation pink
18. Cadmium orange
19. Pale vermillion
20. Yellowed orange
21. Sienna brown
22. Spanish Orange
23. Canary yellow
24. Yellow ochre
25. Golden Rod
26. Metallic gold
27. Parma violet
28. Tuscan Red
29. Mulberry
30. Ultramarine
31. Grey

DESIGN PATTERNS

1. Polka dots
2. Stripes
3. Plaid
4. Floral
5. Chevron
6. Camouflage
7. Animal Pattern
8. Checker
9. Argyle
10. Harlequin
11. Greek Key
12. Gingham
13. Ikat
14. Houndstooth
15. Moroccan
16. Trellis
17. Toile
18. Paisley
19. Tartan
20. Nailshead
21. Tie Dye
22. Moiré
23. Harris Tweed
24. Border tartan
25. Harlequin print
26. African textiles
27. Pinstripes
28. Ise katagami
29. Strawberry Thief
30. Glen Plaid
31. Tattersall

LIGHTING

1. Direct Sunlight: Provides high contrast with harsh highlights and cast shadows.
2. Natural Daylight: using sun as the light source
3. Golden Hour: When the sun is in lower position provides a soft light.
4. Overcast: Cloudy day. There are no shadows and you can see the true colors of the subject.
5. Backlighting/Edge lighting
6. Incandescent Lighting. Warm colour.
7. Fluorescent Lighting
8. LED lighting
9. Tungsten-Halogen Lighting
10. High-density discharge lighting
11. Nightime / Streelights
12. Two sources of lighting
13. Monochrome
14. Sepia
15. Black and white
16. Flat Painting
17. Warm and cool
18. Triadic scheme
19. Color accent
20. Limited Palette
21. Gray and neutrals
22. Spotlighting
23. Reflected light
24. Light from below
25. Contre Jour
26. Frontal lighting
27. Three-Quarter Lighting
28. Occlusion Shadows
29. Half-shadow
30. Hidden light Sources
31. Candlelight

Chapter 12
Stories

I have a proven method to attract people to see your drawings or illustrations: Tell a story. It's a straightforward concept, but sometimes it can be hard to apply to our visual medium. Thinking about a story is a useful and proven method to make your paintings communicate more with your audience and have more impact.

IDEAS TO GET STORIES

1. Use writing prompts
2. Take a photo and make up a story.
3. Reinterpret a classic story.
4. Write a different ending to a well-known story.
5. Pick three unrelated things.
6. Research your favorite author and read his/her biography.
7. Pick a character, a place (setting), and a thing. Pick a random number and search this book for an item in each category. Then, make up a story with these elements.
8. Research the story of a word.
9. Draw a comic about a fairytale.

TYPES OF NARRATIVES

1. Autobiography
2. Biography
3. Captivity narrative
4. Epic
5. Epic poem
6. Essay
7. Fable
8. Folk tale
9. Historical fiction
10. Fantasy
11. Flash fiction
12. Legend
13. Memoir
14. Myth
15. News
16. Nonlinear narrative
17. Novel
18. Novella
19. Parable
20. Play
21. Poem
22. Quest narrative
23. Screenplay
24. Short Story
25. Tall tale

THE CLASSICS

These works of art are considered classics in literature. This list can help you out getting ideas for storybooks, graphic novels or comics.

1. The Gilgamesh (Sumerians)
2. The Iliad by Homer*
3. The Odyssey by Homer
4. Oedipus King by Sophocles
5. The Republic by Platon
6. Poetics by Aristotle
7. Ion by Platon
8. Mahabharata by Unknown (India)
9. Wujing or The Five Classics by Unknown (Zhou period, China)
10. Cicero's speech against Caitilina by Cicero
11. Aeneid by Virgil
12. Amores by Ovid
13. Metamorphoses by Ovid
14. Man youshuo by Unknown (Japan's First anthology of poetry)
15. One Thousand and one Nights or Arabian Nights by Anonymous and Orientalist Antoine Galland
16. Beowulf by Anonymous
17. The Song of Roland by Anonymous (France)
18. The poem of the Cid by Anonymous (Spain)
19. Historia Regum Britanniae by Geoffrey of Monmouth
20. Nibelungenleid by Anonymous
21. The Divine Comedy by Dante Alighieri,
22. The Decameron by Giovanni Boccaccio
23. The Canterbury Tales by Geoffrey Chaucer
24. Il Prince by Niccolò Machiavelli
25. Hamlet by Shakespeare
26. Othello by Shakespeare
27. Shakespeares Sonnets by Shakespeare
28. A Midsummer Nights Dream by Shakespeare
29. Macbeth by Shakespeare
30. Romeo and Juliet by Shakespeare

31. Don Quijote de la mancha by Miguel de Cervantes
32. Paradise Lost by John Milton
33. Gulliver's Travels By Lemuel Gulliver
34. Candide by Voltaire
35. Social Contract by Rosseau
36. Faust by Johann Wolfgang von Goethe,
37. Pride and Prejudice by Jane Austen
38. Emma by Jane Austen
39. Sense and Sensibility by Jane Austen
40. Frankenstein by Mary Shelley
41. The Strange Cases of Dr Jekyll and My Hyde by Robert Louis Stevenson
42. The Hunchback of Notre dame by Victor Hugo
43. Les Miserables by Victor Hugo
44. The Count of Monte Cristo by Alexandre Dumas
45. The Three Musketeers by Alexandre Dumas
46. The Raven By Edgar Allan Poe.
47. Jane Eyre by Charlotte Brontë
48. Wuthering heights by Emily Brontë
49. Walden by Henry David Thoreau
50. Vanity Fair by Condé Nast
51. Little Women by Louisa May Alcott
52. Twenty thousand leagues under the sea by Jules Verne
53. Around the World in eighty days by Jules Verne
54. David Copperfield by Charles Dickens
55. A tales of two cities by Charles Dickens
56. A Christmas carol by Charles Dickens
57. Great expectations by Charles Dickens
58. Oliver Twist by Charles Dickens
59. The Scarlett Letter by Nathaniel Hawthorne
60. Moby Dick by Herman Melville

61. Alice in Wonderland by Lewis Carroll
62. Leaves of Grass by Walt Whitman
63. Madame Bovary by Gustave Flaubert
64. Anna Karenina by Leo Tolstoi
65. War and Peace by Leo Tolstoi
66. Crime and Punishment by Fyodor Dostoevsky
67. The brothers Karamazov by Fyodor Dostoevsky
68. The adventures of tom sawyer by Mark Twain
69. The adventures of huckleberry finn by Mark Twain
70. Tess of the d'Urbervilles by Thomas Hardy
71. Grimm fairy tales by Jacob Grimm and Wilhelm Grimm
72. Dracula by Bram Stoker
73. Treasure Island by Robert Louis Stevenson
74. The Picture of Dorian Grey by Oscar Wilde
75. The Importance of Being Earnest by Oscar Wilde
76. The Adventures of Sherlock Holmes by Arthur Conan Doyl
77. The War of the Worlds by H. G. Wells
78. The Time machine by H. G. Wells
79. The wonderful wizard of oz by L. Frank Baum
80. Anne of Green Gables by Lucy Maud Montgomery
81. The Little Prince by Antoine de Saint-Exupéry
82. The Diary of a Young Girl by Anne Frank
83. The Lord of the Rings by J. R. R. Tolkien.
84. The Secret Garden by Frances Hodgson Burnett
85. Metamorphosis by Franz Kafka
86. Animal Farm by George Orwell
87. 1984 by George Orwell
88. The Mysterious Affair by Agatha Christie
89. Murder at the Orient Express by Agatha Christie
90. The Great Gatsby by F. Scott Fitzgerald

91. Gone with the wind by Margaret Mitchell.
92. Ulysses by James Joyce
93. Mrs Dalloway by Virgina Woolf
94. Of Mice and Men by John Steinbeck
95. The Grapes of Wrath by John Steinbeck
96. The Catcher in the Rye by J. D. Salinger
97. Fahrenheit 451 by Ray Bradbury
98. 100 years of Solitude by Gabriel García Márquez
99. One Flew over the Cuckoo's nest by Miloš Forman
100. To kill a Mockingbird by by Harper Lee

FAIRY TALES

1. Chicken Little (1840)
2. The Golden Mermaid (1892)
3. A Christmas Carol (1843) by Charles Dickens
4. The gingerbread man (1890) by Joseph Jacobs
5. Goldilocks and the Three Bears (1837) by Robert Southey
6. Jack and the Beanstalk (1890) by Joseph Jacobs
7. The Three Little Pigs (1843) by Joseph Jacobs
8. Alice's Adventures in Wonderland (1865) by Lewis Carroll
9. Through the Looking Glass (1871) by Lewis Carrol
10. The Tortoise and the Hare (England)
11. The little Red Hen (19th century English/Russian fairytale)
12. The Elves and the Shoemaker (1812) by Brothers Grimm
13. Golden Goose (1812) by Brothers Grimm
14. Hansel and Gretel (1812) by Brothers Grimm
15. The Nutcracker and the Mouse King by E.T.A. Hoffmann
16. Rapunzel (1812) by Brothers Grimm
17. Rumpelstiltskin (1812) by Brothers Grimm
18. Snow White (1823) by Brothers Grimm
19. Sinbad the Sailor (Before 850) Arabic
20. Aladdin (Before 1709) by Hanna Diyab (One Thousand and One Nights)Arabic
21. Ali baba and the Forty Thieves (Before 1709) By Hanna Diyab
22. Little Red Riding Hood (1695) by Charles Perrault
23. Puss in Boots (1697) by Charles Perrault
24. Sleeping Beauty (1697) by Charles Perrault
25. The Story of Pretty Goldilocks (1698) by Madame d'Aulnoy

26. The Frog Princess by Alexander Afanasyev
27. Pinocchio (1881) by Carlo Collodi
28. Ugly duckling (1843) by Hans Christian Andersen
29. The Red Shoes (1845) by Hans Christian Andersen
30. Thumbelina (1835) by Hans Christian Andersen
31. The little Mermaid (1837) by Hans Christian Andersen
32. The Nightingale (1843) by Hans Christian Andersen
33. The Emperor's New Clothes (1837) by Hans Christian Andersen
34. Sandman (1841) by Hans Christian Andersen
35. The Philosopher's Stone (1859) by Hans Christian Andersen
36. The Snow Queen (1844) by Hans Christian Andersen
37. The Princess and the Pea (1835) by Hans Christian Andersen
38. God Gives a Hundren for one by Americo Paredes
39. The Greenish Bird by Americo Paredes
40. The Tailor who sold his soul to the devil by Americo Paredes
41. Thank God it Wasn't a peso by Americo Paredes

42. The Golden Bracelet by Marie Campbell (1958)
43. Little Cat skin by Marie Campbell (1958)
44. The princess that wore a rabbit-skin dress by Marie Campbell (1958
45. The Tar Baby by Jar Chandler Harris (1881)
46. Br'er Rabbit by Joel Chandler Harris (1881)
47. Br'er Fox and Br'er Bear (African American oral traditions)
48. The laughing place by Joel Chanderl Harris
49. The Boy and the wolves (Native American)
50. The wonderful wizard of ox by L. Frank Baum (1990)

Most Popular Children's Book According to TIME Magazine

1. Where the Wild Things are by Maurice Sendak
2. The Snowy Day by Ezra Jack Keats
3. Goodnight Moon by Margaret Wise Brown
4. Blueberries for Sal, by Robert McCloskey
5. Little Bear (series) by Else Holmelund Minarek
6. Owl Moon by Jane Yolen, Illustrations by John Schoenherr
7. The Giving Tree, by Shel Silverstein
8. The True Story of the Three Little Pigs by Jon Sciezka, illustrations by Lane Smith
9. Tuesday by David Weisner
10. Where the Sidewalk Ends by Shel Silverstein
11. Harold and the Purple Crayon by Crockett Johnson
12. Make Way for Ducklings by Robert McCloskey
13. Olivia by Ian Falconer
14. Madeline (series) by Ludwig Bemelmans
15. Anno's Journey by Mitsumasa Anno

dul Gasazi by Chris Van Allsburg (Houghton Mifflin Harcourt)

16. Frog and Toad (series) by Arnold Lobel
17. Click, Clack, Moo by Doreen Cronin, illustrations by Betsy Lewin.
18. The Story of Ferdinand by Munro Leaf, illustrations by Robert Lawson.
19. Don't Let the Pigeon Drive the Bus, by Mo Williams
20. The Lorax by Dr. Seuss
21. Corduroy, by Don Freeman
22. I Want My Hat Back, by Jon Klassen
23. Miss Rumphius by Barbara Cooney
24. Brave Irene by Willian Steig
25. Alexander and the Terrible, Horrible, No Good, Very Bad Day by Judith Viorst, illustrations by Ray Cruz. (Atheneum Books)
26. The Cat in the Hat by Dr. Seuss (Random House)
27. Press Here by Herve Tullet (Chronicle Books)
28. The Day the Crayons Quit, by Drew Daywalt, illustrations by Oliver Jeffers. (Philomel)
29. Whistle for Willie by Ezra Jack Keats (Puffin)
30. The Garden of Ab

Bibliography

1. Blosser, P.E. (2000). *How to Ask the Right Questions*. National Science Teachers Association.
2. Cameron, J. (2002). *The artist's way: A spiritual path to higher creativity*. New York: J.P. Tarcher/Putnam.
3. Neuburger, Emily K. (2017) *Journal Sparks: Fire Up Your Creativity with Spontaneous Art, Wild Writing, and Inventive Thinking*. North Adams, MA : Storey Publishing.
4. The Disney Imagineers. (2005) *The Imagineering Workout Exercises to Shape Your Creative Muscles by the Disney Imagineers*. Disney Enterprises.Inc.
5. Cameron, J. (2002). *The artist's way: A spiritual path to higher creativity*. New York: J.P. Tarcher/Putnam.
6. The New York Times. (2011) *New York Times Essential Knowledge: A Desk Reference for the Curious Mind*. Macmillan Publishers.
7. Sew Guide. 50+ Different Types of Dresses for Women. (Accessed in 01/17/21) [https://sewguide.com/types-of-dresses/]
8. Sew Guide. *20 types of pants you should definitely own*. (Accessed in 01/17/21) [https://sewguide.com/different-styles-of-pants/]
9. ProFlowers.com. Last updated: March, 19, 2019. 151 *Types of flowers Common in the U.S*. (Accessed in 01/17/21) [https://www.proflowers.com/blog/types-of-flowers]
10. Minerals.net. (No posted date) *Gemstones A-Z*. (Accessed in 17/01/21) [http://www.minerals.net/GemStoneMain.aspx]
11. Anne Helmenstine of Sciencenotes.org (Originally posted in July 28, 2016, Last Updated: September 29, 2020) *Colorful Periodic table with 118 element names*. [https://sciencenotes.org/2016-2017-colorful-periodic-table-118-element-names/]
12. Wikipedia. (Last updated: 28 July, 2017) (accessed in January 17, 2021) *Category: Lists of mammals*. [https://en.wikipedia.org/wiki/Category:Lists_of_mammals]
13. Wikipedia. (Last updated: 23 November 2020) *List of reptiles*. (Last accessed in January 17, 2021) [https://en.wikipedia.org/wiki/List_of_reptiles]
14. Wikipedia. (Last updated : 11 October 2020) *List of fish common names*. (Last accessed: January 17, 2021) [https://en.wikipedia.org/wiki/List_of_fish_common_names]
15. Wikipedia. (Last updated: 4 August, 2013) *Category: Lists of insects*. (Last accessed: January 17, 2021) [https://en.wikipedia.org/wiki/Category:Lists_of_insects]
16. Wikipedia. (Last updated: 14 January, 2021) *Crustacean* (Last accessed: January 17, 2021) [https://en.wikipedia.org/wiki/Crustacean]
17. Wikipedia. Myriapoda. 1/8/21 (Accessed in 01/17/21) https://en.wikipedia.org/wiki/Myriapoda]

18.   Wikipedia. (Last updated: 6 January 2021) *List of bicycle types*. (Last Accessed in 17/01/21) [https://en.wikipedia.org/wiki/List_of_bicycle_types]

19.   Navy Recruiting Command. Last updated. 1/4/21 *Navy Vessels*. (Accessed in 01/17/21) [https://www.navy.com/about/equipment/vessels/submarines.html]

20.   Wings over Kansas.com (Posted: April, 26, 2009) *Different kinds and types of Aircrafts*. (Accessed in 17/01/21) [http://www.wingsoverkansas.com/features/a1037/]

21.   Wikipedia. (Last updated: 20 November 2020) *List of aircraft by date and usage category*. (Last Accessed in 17 January, 2021) [https://en.wikipedia.org/wiki/List_of_aircraft_by_date_and_usage_category]

22.   Wikipedia. (Last Updated: 20 December 2020)*Train* (Last Accessed in 17January, 2021) https://en.wikipedia.org/wiki/Train]

23.   Wikipedia. Last Updated: 11 January 2021 . *List of Asian countries*. (Last Accessed in 17 January, 2021) [https://en.wikipedia.org/wiki/List_of_Asian_countries_by_area]

24.   Wikipedia. (Last Updated: 29 December 2020) *List of African countries by area* (Last Accessed in 17 January, 2021) [https://en.wikipedia.org/wiki/List_of_African_countries_by_area]

25.   Wikipedia. (Last Updated: 21 December 2020) *List of North American countries by area* (Last Accessed in 17 January, 2021) [https://en.wikipedia.org/wiki/List_of_North_American_countries_by_area]

26.   Wikipedia. (Last Updated : 4 January, 2021) *List of South American Countries by area*. (Last Accessed in 17 January, 2021) [https://en.wikipedia.org/wiki/List_of_South_American_countries_by_area]

27.   Wikipedia. *Apollo 13*. (Accessed in 01/17/21) [https://en.wikipedia.org/wiki/Apollo_13]

28.   Wikipedia. (Last updated: January 15, 2021) *Public holidays in the United States* (Last accessed : 17/01/21) [https://en.wikipedia.org/wiki/Public_holidays_in_the_United_States#Holidays_most_commonly_celebrated]

29.   Wikipedia. (Last Updated: 4 January, 2021) *List of Oceanian countries by area* (Last Accessed in 17 January, 2021) https://en.wikipedia.org/wiki/List_of_Oceanian_countries_by_area]

30. TIME. (By the editors of TIME, with reporting by Daniel D'Addario, Girl Nathan and Noah Rayman) (Last Accessed 17/01/21) *The List: 100 Best Children's Books of All Time* [(https://time.com/100-best-childrens-books/]

31. Wikipedia. (Last Updated: 12 January, 2021) *List of narrative forms*. Last Accessed 17 January, 2021 https://en.wikipedia.org/wiki/List_of_narrative_forms

32. Gurney, James (2010) *Color and Light*. Andrews McMeel Publishing.

www.ingramcontent.com/pod-product-compliance
Lightning Source LLC
Chambersburg PA
CBHW050005230526
45465CB00003BB/1266